HOTEL AND CATERING
COSTING AND BUDGETS

HOTEL AND CATERING
COSTING AND BUDGETS

R. D. Boardman
F.C.A.

Dorset Institute of
Higher Education

HEINEMANN : LONDON

William Heinemann Ltd
10 Upper Grosvenor Street, London W1X 9PA

LONDON MELBOURNE TORONTO
JOHANNESBURG AUCKLAND

First published 1969
Second edition 1972
Reprinted 1975
Third edition 1978
Reprinted 1980

434 90158 X

Printed and bound in Great Britain by
Fakenham Press Limited, Fakenham, Norfolk

Contents

Preface by the author

THIS book has been written primarily for students taking courses in hotel and catering management, having regard to the requirements of the following examinations:

(a) Intermediate and Final Membership examinations of the Hotel, Catering and Institutional Management Association, *(b)* The Ordinary National Diploma in Hotel and Catering Operations, *(c)* The Ordinary National Diploma in Institutional Housekeeping and Catering, *(d)* The Higher National Diploma in Catering and Hotel Management, and *(e)* The Higher National Diploma in Institutional Management.

With this object in view the questions at the end of each chapter have been chosen to develop ideas expressed in the text, and a chapter has been included containing quick revision notes.

It is hoped that the book will also be of value to managers or proprietors in the industry who are not able to call on the services of a qualified accountant for day-to-day financial information.

My thanks are due to the H.C.I., now the H.C.I.M.A., for permission to include questions from past examinations. The solutions given at the end of the book are my own.

Currency less than £1 is written as 5p for isolated amounts, or £0·05 when forming part of a calculation. Liquid measures are expressed in litres (l.) divided into 10 decilitres (dl). Weights are expressed in kilograms (kg) divided into 1,000 grams (g).

Preface to the 3rd Edition

INCREASING costs, and the general fall in the value of currency, result in money amounts being higher each year than they were the year before. The principles and method of costing remain the same, but familiar values change.

In this edition the figures in the examples and questions have been revised so that the results will look more realistic, but as is emphasized in Chapter 1, costing is a continuous process and constant application of the method will take care of changes in basic prices.

Additional chapters have been included dealing with marginal costing, and standard costing, which are not new topics, but are new to examinations for hotel and catering students.

As before, sample exercises have been included in order to develop the ideas expressed in the text.

1. *Introduction*

COSTING may be defined as ascertaining the costs relating to a suitable unit of output. In catering the unit may be one of *production* (e.g. a dish to be served), it may be an *event* (e.g. a banquet), or it may be a unit of *time* (e.g. a month). In a hotel costs may be expressed as so much 'per sleeper night'.

A hotelier or caterer will want his business to make a profit, which means that the charges he makes to customers must be more than sufficient to cover all his costs. In order to satisfy himself that this is happening he will need to see that the volume of his sales is maintained at a sufficiently high level, and that the costs and sales maintain the correct relationship to each other.

Anyone selling goods or services of whatever kind will have made calculations of this sort, if only mentally, but few businesses are sufficiently free from complexities for inspired guesswork to result in a profit over a period of time. It is necessary to tackle the question systematically so as to leave as little as possible to chance in determining the relationship of costs to sales. Only in this way will unprofitable ventures be detected in time to correct or abandon them before damage is done. *prices changing all the time*

Costing is a continuous process, and the different units of measurement are interrelated. Before selling is begun it is necessary to find out the cost of the goods and services to be sold in order to determine what selling price will be necessary to cover the cost and leave a profit. Calculations will be made of the costs relating to each dish, and these calculations must be repeated under working conditions to check actual performance against expected results. Changes in basic food prices will necessitate recalculation, and with the passing of time calculations of the actual costs of the business as a whole will be made regularly as a check on overall profitability.

It should not be thought that it is sufficient to ascertain the cost of the food supplied to customers. Although food cost will undoubtedly be the largest single item of cost in a restaurant, other costs which are not so obvious will probably add up to more than the cost of food. However, food cost is a major cost which has the advantage of being readily ascertained, and may therefore be dealt with separately.

Because of difficulties in determining certain costs for particular units of sales it is seldom practicable to deal with all costs in one calculation. Some division into component parts enables the problem to be tackled systematically, and for this purpose it is useful to break down total cost into groups, each group comprising costs of a similar type.

All this may lead one to suppose that costing involves a large staff, and that the 'cost of costing' may be more than a small business can afford. Nothing could be further from the truth. Certainly it is true that many large concerns employ considerable staffs engaged only on costing, but it should not be thought that a small concern will need a great deal of work to produce information adequate for its needs. The principles involved will be the same for any business, but the quantity of detail necessary will be relative to the size of business. Rather should the question be, 'can I afford *not* to have properly costed figures?', since lack of accurate information on profitability so easily leads to failure.

That there is an increasing awareness of this in the hotel and catering industry is apparent from the interest shown in the subject, particularly by proprietors of smaller hotels and restaurants. These are far and away more numerous than the larger organizations, yet in the past have usually had no costing system in use, and in many cases this situation is still true. The larger organizations employ their own accountants who will prepare the required information for management, but in the smaller concern, the proprietor will probably have to be satisfied with what he can do himself.

Literature on the subject of costing and management accounting is readily available, but hitherto it has been almost exclusively concerned with other industries, notably engineering and printing. The application of such books to hotels and restaurants has been a difficult matter for proprietors and students alike, and since any attempt at serious financial control depends on the proprietor's own knowledge for the greater part of the industry, it is not surprising that the attempt is so seldom constructive.

It is with these needs in mind that the following chapters have been written, and it is hoped that the result will prove of practical use to both students and 'do-it-yourself' proprietors. In considering descriptions of methods or systems, however, it should be emphasized that adaptation to individual businesses will be required. No two businesses are exactly alike, and no detailed system of costing will be entirely suitable for all businesses. The method used in any business should be the one most suited to that business, which means that it must be the *simplest* way of obtaining the required information. Simplicity leads to speedy information in normal times, and in times of stress it may well mark the difference between speedy information and no information at all.

EXERCISES
1. What is costing? Why is it necessary?
2. What is meant by a 'unit of sales'? Give three examples.
3. Explain the expression 'the cost of costing'.
4. 'A job well done is done for ever.' Discuss this in relation to costing.

a good foundation in good costing will always be there but of course it will change all the time

2. Elements of Sales and Costs

THE amount received from sales must be sufficient to pay for all costs and leave something over as profit for the proprietor of the business. This profit is known as *net profit*, and must be distinguished from *gross profit* which is the amount left out of sales when only the cost of goods sold has been deducted. In the hotel and catering industry, gross profit is taken to mean sales less food cost.

The total costs may be broken down into three main headings, food cost, labour cost, and overheads, referred to as the elements of cost.

Food cost is the cost of material used in producing the food sold.

Labour cost is the cost of employing staff, and will include wages, salaries, the value of staff meals supplied, and the value of staff accommodation where applicable. The term wages itself should include not only the gross pay from the weekly payroll but also petty cash payments for casual labour, and the employer's contributions to National Insurance and Graduated Pensions.

Overheads are those items of expense not falling under the headings of food cost or labour cost, and will include such things as rent, gas and electricity, advertising, depreciation of equipment, etc.

If we regard our sales as a cake to be divided up between payments for various costs and net profit for the proprietor it would look something like Figure 1 on p. 6.

Food Cost is shaded in the diagram, and when this has been taken out the remainder which is unshaded is the *gross profit*. Out of this, labour cost and overheads must be paid for, and what is left is *net profit*. Conversely it follows that:

net profit + overheads + labour cost = gross profit

This is important to remember when some elements of cost are unknown, and it becomes necessary to estimate the unknown factors by calculation of the proportions by reference to the known factors. Thus the cost of food can always be calculated, but exact calculation of labour and overheads relating to a small unit of sales may be impossible. However, if we can establish the ratio of the various elements to each other it is a matter of simple arithmetic to calculate an unknown amount from the ratio it bears to a known amount. This is achieved by expressing each element of sales as a *percentage of sales.*

COMPARISONS AND PERCENTAGES

If we look at the accounts of a restaurant for a month they might look something like this:

		£	
Sales		6,000	100%
Food cost		2,400	40%
Gross profit		3,600	60%
Labour cost:			
Kitchen	875		
Restaurant	800	1,675	28%
Overheads:			
Rent and rates	450		
Lighting and heating	150		
Printing and stationery	50		
Insurance	25		
Repairs and maintenance	100		
Sundry expenses	200		
Depreciation	150	1,125	19%
		2,800	47%
Net profit		800	13%

The amounts themselves are of only passing interest until they are compared with something else. Knowing that overheads amounted to £1,125 tells us very little of importance. The amount may be high for this type of business or it may be quite low. If we had the relative figures for the same month last year, they would immediately be more useful by comparison.

However any increase or reduction compared with last year may

Pie Chart.

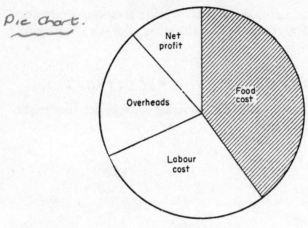

Figure 1

be due to the amount of business done being different from last year, and we allow for this by expressing each figure as a percentage of sales. Thus the overheads this year are seen to be 19%, or £19 for every £100 of sales. If last year the overheads were 20% of sales, even though the *amount* this year may be more, the ratio to sales is less, and the business is therefore more profitable.

Applying this method to all the figures we see that the elements of sales can be expressed as definite proportions, which in this example are:

100%
{
Food cost   40%
Labour cost   28%
Overheads   19%
Net profit   13%
} Gross profit 60%

It will be seen that for this business a gross profit of 60% of sales was needed to cover labour cost, overheads, and net profit. If the sales level altered materially the proportions would be different, because certain of the expenses to be covered by the gross profit will remain the same amount whatever the level of sales. For this level of sales, however, the proportion needed is 60%, and it may be assumed that provided the level of output remained the same, this result could have been ensured if each unit of sales during the month was calculated to produce a 60% gross profit. Put in another way, this means that if the food cost of each dish sold was 40% of the selling price, then the result for the month would be as above.

It will probably be true that the proportions of costs for this one month will not hold good for every month. Seasonal variations will occur in, for example, fuel oil consumption for heating the premises. The amount of sales will vary, causing changes in the percentages of those expenses which do not vary, such as rates. However if the proportions are established for a period of a year, so that we can say, for example, that a gross profit of 60% was needed to cover costs and net profit for the year, then a 60% gross profit achieved on every dish sold throughout the year would produce the desired result at the end of the year whatever the seasonal variations in expense proportions.

SALES VOLUME

In any consideration of costs as a proportion of sales, it is necessary to consider the volume of sales. Many items of cost do not vary as a result of increasing or reducing sales, with the result that proportions will change as a result of changing sales volume. If the volume of sales is very low, it may be that total costs will not be covered however much care is taken in controlling those costs which do vary. If sales are very high, on the other hand, the proportionate effect of fixed costs will be less and the net profit achieved will be a higher percentage of sales although the variable costs are maintained at a constant percentage.

SALES MIX

The expression *sales mix* refers to the composition of total sales, when these comprise items of different kinds, e.g.

	Percentage of total sales
Food sales	78
Beverage	20
Other	2
Total sales	100%

The different kinds of sales produce different proportionate profits, so that an increase or reduction in *one kind* of sales will not produce a proportionate alteration in *total* profit.

In an hotel, total takings may include food and beverage sales, accommodation charges, bar sales, and other takings. Food sales may comprise residents' meals and chance meals, which may be priced differently. *Table d'hôte* meals may be priced differently from *à la carte* meals. All these differences will have their effect on considerations of increases or reductions in cost, and must be borne in mind when forecasts are made of future results.

HIGH AND LOW MARGIN RETURN

The figure of 60% used above is merely an example which is convenient for illustration, but it is nevertheless a percentage which is accepted as generally reasonable for the gross profit of a restaurant. The gross profit returned by a business when expressed as a percentage of sales is commonly referred to as the *margin*, and a higher than normal gross profit percentage is said to be a *high margin return*. Similarly a lower than normal gross profit percentage is said to be a *low margin return*.

Individual concerns may work on percentages as low as 55%, or as high as 65%, depending on circumstances. Since the gross profit has to pay for labour cost, overheads, and net profit, the circumstances affecting the rate, or percentage, of gross profit will be those affecting these three elements of sales. A high rate of gross profit does not necessarily betoken a high net profit, nor does a low rate of gross profit necessarily entail losses.

The chain store concept of low margin and high turnover is an example of this. The gross profit percentage, or margin, can be kept low because turnover is so high that expenses are *comparatively* low, and all percentages are comparisons. The expenses may be high, and gross profit higher, when expressed in £s. But when expressed as a percentage of the very high turnover, they appear to be smaller percentages than would be expected in other businesses.

In considering two restaurants, one with a gross profit of 55%, and one with 65%, no conclusions should be drawn without more information. It may be that the respective proprietors are receiving similar amounts of net profit for similar amounts of turnover, but have just organized their businesses differently:

		Restaurant A		Restaurant B
Sales		£25,000		£25,000
Gross profit	(55%)	13,750	(65%)	16,250
Labour cost	(24%)	6,000	(30%)	7,500
Overheads	(21%)	5,250	(25%)	6,250
		11,250		13,750
Net profit	(10%)	£2,500	(10%)	£2,500

With this additional information, some idea can be gained of the types of restaurant involved. It looks as though one restaurant may be of a luxury type, with considerable staff and heavy overheads, while the other is of the more popular type. It should be obvious which is which.

REPRESENTATIVE CUSTOMER

If this interpretation is correct, it will probably be true that the sales of restaurant A are made up of a considerable number of meals of comparatively small amount, while the sales of restaurant B consist of fewer sales of larger amount. It is frequently very informative to know the amount of the *average meal*, or as it is sometimes expressed, the *representative customer,* and the method is to divide the total sales by the number of meals served. Thus in the above example, we may find that the sales of restaurant A comprised 25,000 meals, while restaurant B sold 10,000 meals. Since the total value of sales is £25,000 in both cases, it means that the representative customer spends £1·00 in restaurant A, and £2·50 in restaurant B.

REWARD FOR CAPITAL INVESTED

The two restaurants quoted in the above example have the same amount of sales, and ultimately produce the same net profit. For the comparison to be valid, however, it should be ascertained that the profit quoted really is net. One factor which is seldom taken into account in calculating net profit for the purposes of annual financial accounts is interest on the capital invested, but for critical comparison purposes it would be misleading to ignore it.

The proprietor of restaurant *A* may have invested £10,000 in his business, while the proprietor of restaurant *B* has invested £20,000. Allowance for this disparity must be made in comparing the profitability of the two concerns, because there would otherwise be no reward to proprietor *B* to induce him to provide the extra capital. For the profit of £2,500 to be considered equal in each case, it must be calculated after charging interest on the capital invested, at a normal rate of interest. If 10% is considered a reasonable rate, then the amount of overheads for restaurant *A* should include £1,000 (10% of £10,000 invested) as interest on capital invested, and the overheads of restaurant *B* should include £2,000 (10% of £20,000).

If the capital has been borrowed, from a bank for example, this interest will have to be paid to the lender, and will be included in the figure of overheads as a matter of course. When the proprietor invests his own money in the business, however, it is not always realized that the equivalent of such interest should be produced by the business before it can be said to have produced a net profit. If the proprietor has £20,000 to invest, he could invest it in government stocks to produce 10% without all the risks and worry attendant on a business. For the business to be attractive, it must produce equivalent interest *plus* additional profit.

PROPRIETOR'S REMUNERATION

Net profit should be regarded as a proprietor's reward for *engaging* in business, without considering whether he also *manages* the day-to-day running of the business. This is a separate function for which a separate manager might be engaged at a salary, or for which the proprietor should expect to obtain a salary in addition to proprietor's profit. The principle is similar to the inclusion of interest on capital; in both cases something belonging to the proprietor, capital or labour, is being put into the business, which would otherwise need to be bought from someone else. In considering the profitability of the business, an allowance must be made in either case.

HOTELS

In hotels, the takings comprise sales of food as in a restaurant, plus charges for letting accommodation. The first are sales producing a gross profit, after charging the cost of food sold, while the latter are charges having no direct material cost, and the question of gross profit is inapplicable. There may also be various other sources of revenue, such as a bar, or garage charges, some of which will be of one kind and some of the other.

The important fact to recognize here is that we are in effect dealing with two kinds of business, even though customers may be charged an inclusive amount to cover both kinds. For costing purposes it may be possible to deal with both aspects together, but where this causes difficulty the answer is to separate the costing information for each section of the business. This will be dealt with more fully in later chapters.

COMPOSITION OF FOOD COST AND KITCHEN PERCENTAGES

The cost of the different kinds of food included in the total food cost will usually remain fairly consistently in the same proportions, so that if each item of food is expressed as a percentage of total food cost, regular comparison of these percentages each week will draw attention to unusual variations. If the gross profit percentage appears low at any time, then examination of the food-cost composition may reveal the cause.

Variations may be due to:
1. Increases in purchase price of some commodities.
2. Changes in sales composition (e.g. fall in sales of roasts and increased sales of salads in hot weather).
3. Wastage.
4. Pilfering.
5. Lack of portion control.
6. Bad buying.
7. Overcharging by suppliers.
8. Clerical errors.

In each case some action should be taken in order to ensure that the business remains profitable, and the variation in percentage is an indication that something requires investigation. In the case of (1) and (2) above, the reasons are normal external changes, but they still need to be recognized and acted upon. Increases in purchase price may well call for increases in selling price. Whether charges are increased or not must be considered, so that future action is deliberate and there is not inaction due to ignorance. In the case of changes in sales composition the need for care in re-ordering is highlighted.

In the other cases the reason is some kind of inefficiency in running the business, in each case resulting in some particular kind of food becoming exceptionally expensive. For example, if a supplier charges for larger quantities than were actually delivered, the relative cost of that commodity will increase and will be indicated by a higher percentage of total food cost.

As an alternative to expressing each item as a percentage of total food cost, these detailed food costs may be expressed as a percentage of sales, so that the individual percentages add up to the total food cost percentage of sales instead of adding to 100% of total food cost. In either case the comparison with other periods is the important thing, so the method adopted must be consistent.

Example

The kitchen analysis sheets for the weeks ended 22 May and 29 May showed goods consumed as follows:

	W/E 22 May		W/E 29 May	
	£	%	£	%
Meat	35	14·0	41	13·7
Poultry	20	8·0	23	7·7
Fish	11	4·4	13	4·3
Fruit and vegetables	28	11·2	40	13·3
Grocery	45	18·0	53	17·7
Provisions	48	19·2	57	19·0
Bread, flour, etc.	18	7·2	21	7·0
Milk and cream	25	10·0	29	9·7
Eggs	14	5·6	16	5·3
Sundries	6	2·4	7	2·3
	£250	100·0%	£300	100·0%

It will be seen that every percentage for the week ended 29 May is slightly less than the previous week except for fruit and vegetables, which is 13·3% of the total instead of 11·2%. The reason for this should be sought, so that correcting action may be taken if necessary.

Gross Profit = Sales — Food Cost
or
Labour Cost + Ohdet Net Profit

EXERCISES

1. What are the elements of sales?
2. What are the elements of cost?
3. What is meant by 'the inclusive cost of labour'?
4. List six items of overhead expense.
5. Explain the terms gross profit and net profit.
6. The sales of a restaurant in July amount to £5,250; food cost is £2,100, labour cost is £1,575, and overheads are £1,050. What net profit has been made?
7. The cost of employing staff in a restaurant is expected to be £18,000 for next year, and overheads will amount to £10,500. What gross profit must be achieved in order to make a net profit of £6,000? If sales amount to £60,000, what is the gross profit percentage of sales?
8. Calculate the gross profit percentage of sales for each of the following:
    (a) Sales £8,550; food cost £3,150; labour cost £2,250; overheads £1,650.
    (b) Food cost £13,120; labour cost £8,320; overheads £6,560; net profit £4,000.
    (c) Sales £9,300; labour cost £2,232; overheads £2,604; net profit £1,023.
9. Why are costs and profit frequently expressed as a percentage of sales?
10. Why is it important to establish a rate of gross profit?
11. Explain the terms high margin return and low margin return, and give examples of the circumstances in which each of them might be accepted as reasonable.
12. What is meant by the representative customer?
13. The takings of a restaurant in May amounted to £7,029; food cost was £2,775, labour cost was £1,809, and overheads were £1,695. 3,905 meals were served during the month.
    Calculate:
    (a) The value of the representative customer.
    (b) The representative customer's contribution to the net profit of the business.
14. The following table shows the food-cost composition of the Elite Restaurant for three successive weeks:

	April 4 £	April 11 £	April 18 £
Meat	161	188	168
Fish and poultry	193	200	232
Fruit and vegetables	116	112	135
Groceries	132	140	137
Dairy	77	80	116
Bakery	54	55	58
Tea and coffee	39	41	40

(a) Express each item as a percentage of total food cost for the week.

(b) Comment on the food-cost composition of each week.

3. Dish Costing

FOR each dish to be served it is necessary to calculate what charge to the customer will, if the volume of sales is maintained, cover all costs and leave an adequate net profit. Unless this is done the question of making a profit is left to chance, and may very well result in making a loss.

This is not to say that the selling price thus calculated fixes the price to be charged. Ultimately the price to be charged is governed by what the customer is willing to pay, and the costing calculation may merely demonstrate that the dish is uneconomic to serve. This itself is very important to know, particularly with seasonal foods when food costs fluctuate considerably. In these cases it will be economic to serve the dish perhaps only for a week or two, and the point at which rising costs make it uneconomic must be known.

GROSS PROFIT PERCENTAGE

The question of what charge will cover all costs and an adequate net profit presents certain problems when applied to a small unit of sales such as one dish, the principal problem being to find out how much the costs and net profit amount to. The cost of the food itself can be calculated with reasonable accuracy, by listing all the ingredients with their individual prices, and then adding up the cost of all the ingredients

In order to reach any conclusion as to the food cost of the dish, it must be clear what is being costed. The article named must be the same article every time it is produced, and this means using a *standard recipe*, so that the same ingredients are always used. Similarly the same quantity of ingredients must consistently produce the same number of served portions by adherence to a system of portion control. This will be dealt with more fully in Chapter 6.

When we come to labour cost, however, the matter is not quite so easy. If one member of staff alone performed all the functions necessary to prepare and serve the dish, and if he worked on no other dish during that time, it might be possible to calculate the time taken at the appropriate rate of pay, and arrive at the labour cost of the dish. In practice, of course, many people will be involved in some way to varying degrees, and not one will have devoted his time exclusively to this particular dish. Consequently any attempt to calculate the value of labour cost exactly will be time-consuming, frustrating, and inaccurate.

Similarly, overheads and net profit will be difficult to determine with any degree of certainty, but they must be covered by the charge to the customer, so some means must be found to evaluate them. The answer is to stop thinking of each cost in terms of 'how much', and to think instead of 'what proportion', that is, the proportion of the charge to the customer which will be needed to cover these costs and net profit. The charge to the customer we refer to as *sales*, and the proportion of sales will be expressed as a percentage. If we can express each element of sales as a percentage of sales, and we know the amount of one of the elements (food cost), then we shall be able to calculate exactly the sales and other costs which are in the correct proportion to the known food cost. In practice, we will reduce the amount of calculation by dealing with labour cost, overheads, and net profit together under the heading 'gross profit'.

It then becomes necessary to decide what percentage of sales the gross profit will need to be. We want to know this in connection with our costs and price-fixing of individual dishes, but the percentage, or proportion, can be taken to be the same as that shown by previous accounts of profit. If last year's profit and loss account shows a gross profit of 60% of sales, and every unit of sales in the forthcoming year is priced to produce a gross profit of 60%, then we may expect the total gross profit achieved this year to be 60% of the year's sales.

In fact, the gross profit percentage actually achieved will be less than that used in the dish-costing calculations because of the effect of wastage of one sort or another. How much less it will be varies from business to business, and in a seasonal business it will vary from season to season. In this connection 'wastage' includes complying with the customer who demands extra helpings, dishes costed to give a low margin, and delay in amending costings to include increased buying prices, in addition to the more obvious forms of wastage.

The difference between the costing gross profit percentage and that actually achieved should not be great, and the amount for each business will be found by experience. If the difference is great, then something has gone wrong which should be investigated immediately,

$$\frac{Gross\ Profit \times 100}{Sales} = G.P\ \%.$$

but generally it will be found to be within 1 or 2%. For the purposes of illustration, we will ignore this difference and assume that the gross profit percentage achieved on every dish will be achieved by the business as a whole over a period.

CALCULATIONS

If it is estimated that a gross profit of 60% of sales is required to cover labour cost, overheads, and net profit, then food cost must be 40% of sales. The value of food cost can be exactly calculated, and from this the required selling price to give a 60% gross profit can be found from the following formula:

$$\text{selling price} = \frac{\text{food cost} \times 100}{40}$$

Thus if the ingredients of a dish cost £0·20 and a gross profit of 60% is to be obtained, then £0·20 represents 40% of the required selling price, which will be:

$$\frac{£0·20 \times 100}{40} = £0·50$$

With a selling price of £0·50 and food cost of £0·20 the gross profit is £0·30, and this is 60% of £0·50.

If a gross profit of 55% is thought to be sufficient, then the food cost will be 45% and the formula for finding the required selling price will be:

$$\text{selling price} = \frac{\text{food cost} \times 100}{45}$$

Using the same example of ingredients costing £0·20, the required selling price would be:

$$\frac{£0·20 \times 100}{45} = £0·444$$

The calculations follow the same sequence whatever the percentages used:

1. Determine what gross profit percentage is required to cover labour cost, overheads, and the required net profit; that is, what proportion of sales these amount to.

2. Find the amount of the food cost of the dish. This will be dealt with below.
3. Subtract the gross profit percentage from 100 in order to find the food cost percentage. Since food cost and gross profit together equal total sales, their percentages of sales must together equal 100% of sales.
4. Divide the amount of food cost by the food cost percentage and multiply by 100, in order to find the selling price:

$$\text{selling price} = \frac{\text{food cost} \times 100}{\text{food cost percentage}}$$

Standard
Receipe Card more COSTING SHEETS
usual.

At this stage it is necessary to consider how to calculate the food cost for a dish. The first essential is to prepare a list of all the ingredients necessary to prepare the dish in a convenient quantity, e.g. sufficient for four covers. Prices for each ingredient should then be checked with the invoices and the values calculated.

For those ingredients which are purchased the prices may be obtained from suppliers' invoices or price lists. But some items may not have been purchased, but have been made up in the kitchen, such as stock, sauces, pastry, etc. In these cases in order to insert the appropriate price on a dish costing it will first be necessary to prepare a costing of the particular ingredient.

Simple addition will then give the total food cost for four covers, which should be divided by four to ascertain the cost per cover. All this is made very much easier if it is set out in an organized way, and it is convenient to use standard *costing sheets* which can be prepared in advance and afterwards filed away for reference. (*See* Figure 2.)

It is important that the date of costing should be shown, as a guide to its being out of date when referred to later. The quantity being costed must also be clearly indicated, to ensure that it will be possible to calculate the cost per portion.

Where the costing is for a complete dish, the quantity will be expressed as so many portions. Where the costing is for, say, chipped potatoes, the quantity will be expressed as so many grams weight, and to calculate the cost per portion it will also be necessary to specify the size of portion being costed.

Such items as seasoning, parsley, bay leaves, etc., should be allowed for at an estimated cost for the whole, where each item is too small to value individually. Bearing in mind that a gross profit of 60% means that the selling price is 2½ times the food cost, then ½p extra food cost will add more than 1p to the calculated selling price, so a minimum calculation unit of £0·001 is advisable.

COSTING SHEET

Date *10 April* 19__

Name of dish *Irish Stew*

Costing for *4 Portions* Quantity

Qty	Unit	Ingredients	Price £	Unit	Cost £
600	g	Stewing Lamb	1·05	Kg	0·630
500	g	Potatoes	0·33	Kg	0·165
100	g	Onions	0·46	Kg	0·046
100	g	Celery	0·47	Kg	0·047
100	g	White of Leeks	0·56	Kg	0·056
100	g	Button Onions	0·59	Kg	0·059
		Seasoning etc.	0·01		0·010
Total food cost					1·013
Food cost per portion (size)					0·253
Gross profit %					60%
Selling price per portion					0·633
Charge					64p

① F/C per Portion = £0·253 x2·5 = 5p = 63p

② £0·253 ÷ 150 = = 5p(60%) = £0·63p

Figure 2. A dish costing sheet

Costing sheets prepared in this way, for each dish served, form a record of food costs covering the entire range of dishes and can easily be referred to for re-checking when there is any material change in prices. It should again be emphasized that a costing once done is *not* done for ever, but needs to be revised regularly.

CHANGES IN COST PERCENTAGES

As an example of this let us look at the costing for *Irish Stew* illustrated in Figure 2, which was costed in April 19...If in November the price of stewing lamb had increased to £1·20 per kg, the cost of other ingredients being the same, then the total food cost for four portions would be £1·103 and the food cost per portion £0·276. If the charge to the customer remains at 64p then the gross profit now being made is only 57%.

For the dish to produce a gross profit of 60% with the increased cost it will be necessary to calculate a revised selling price. Once again food cost will be 40% of the new selling price, and this new selling price, calculated as before, amounts to £0·690:

$$\text{selling price} = \frac{\text{food cost} \times 100}{\text{food cost percentage}}$$
$$= \frac{£0·276 \times 100}{40}$$
$$= £0·690$$

A common error is to attempt to adjust the original selling price by the amount of alteration in percentage. In the above example, having discovered that the increase in cost has resulted in a gross profit of 57% instead of 60%, it must not be thought that the remedy is to increase the selling price 64p by 3%. It must be remembered that percentages are not absolute numbers, but *expressions of proportion* related to sales, and if the selling price is to be increased, the percentages will be percentages of the *new* selling price. Instead of trying to adjust previous figures, the full formula should be set out as above using the new food cost to find the new selling price.

Similarly it may be that a change in the gross profit percentage is required, perhaps to cover increased overheads, and a new selling price is to be calculated although the food cost remains unaltered.

Example

The food cost of a portion of *Sole Colbert* is £0·99, and it is sold for £2·54, which produces a gross profit of 61%. The proprietor decides that a gross profit of 65% is necessary, and it is desired to know what increase in selling price will achieve this.

Answer

The reference to an increase in price should not be allowed to confuse the issue. The basic facts are that the food cost is £0·99, and the food cost percentage is to be 35% (100—65%). Now,

$$\text{selling price} = \frac{\text{food cost} \times 100}{\text{food cost percentage}}$$
$$= \frac{£0·99 \times 100}{35}$$
$$= £2·829$$

Now that we know the new selling price we can find the increase by subtraction:

$$\text{Increase in selling price} = £2·829 - £2·54 = £0·289$$

The amounts have been shown correct to the nearest £0·001, although such a price as £2·829 would never appear on the menu. The question of whether the menu price should be £2·80, £2·83, or £2·85 is a matter of management policy, decided in the light of the costing information and other matters such as competitors' prices. For the costing information to be useful to management in making the decision, it must be reasonably exact. If there is doubt about whether the costing figure has already been approximated, its usefulness has gone immediately.

PRICING POLICY AND SUPPLEMENT

Once we have ascertained the economic ratio between our food cost and sales, we may adopt a policy of fixing our charges by relating the charge for each dish to its food cost. For this purpose we may find the calculations easier if the selling price is expressed as being so much per cent more than food cost, the percentage used being a percentage of food cost. We have already seen that to achieve a gross profit of 60% of sales, the selling price needs to be

$$\frac{\text{food cost} \times 100}{40}$$

As a calculation of selling price this formula is cumbersome, and the same result will be obtained by expressing the selling price as:

$$\text{food cost} + 150\% \text{ of food cost}$$

This addition to food cost for determining selling price is referred to as the *supplement*, and is always expressed as a percentage of food cost. Its use is purely for calculating selling price from a known food cost, and is in no way a change in the use of percentages of sales for comparison purposes.

FIXING THE MENU PRICE

In fixing the menu price, consideration should be given to the calculated selling price arrived at by increasing ingredient cost by a constant percentage, and in many cases the answer thus arrived at will be satisfactory and may be included in the menu. It is unwise, however, to follow this method blindly without considering any other factors.

Despite all calculations of what gross profit percentage is required to cover labour cost, overheads, and net profit for a given volume of sales, it frequently happens that menu prices are fixed for certain items which give a different gross profit percentage. Considerations of competitors' prices, policy decisions regarding promotion of certain lines, or a simple alteration of an exactly calculated selling price to the nearest round figure may all result in charging a price which does not give the generally aimed-for percentage.

In some cases it may be that the costs involved are not so high as in other cases, and a lower gross profit percentage will be sufficient to cover the remaining costs and profit. Consider, for instance, bread rolls and pre-portioned butter pats. If the rolls are purchased from outside bakers, the food cost includes all preparation costs, leaving only labour cost for restaurant service and general overheads to be paid for out of gross profit. Similarly fresh fruit may warrant pricing to give a different percentage gross profit from prepared dishes. The overall gross profit must still cover labour cost, overheads, and net profit, but individual items, or *groups* of items, may be priced to give different percentages.

MEAL COSTING

When it is necessary to cost a complete meal, as for example in the case of a *table d'hôte* luncheon, it may be attempted by treating the whole meal as one big dish for costing purposes, listing all the ingredients from soup to dessert.

However, the costing sheets of the individual courses should already be available, and the meal costs will then be found by adding the individual dish costs together. This has the great advantage of flexibility, enabling the management to choose dishes of the right cost to be offered for each course, and making it possible to give the customer a choice of different dishes within the framework of the total price.

EXERCISES

Note: In the following questions all calculations of cost should be given correct to £0·001, and percentages correct to one decimal place. For question 8 onwards, use the price list at the end of these exercises.

1. The following quantities are required for twelve covers of *Filet de Sole Bonne Femme:*   100g - kg.

6 × 500 g	Dover soles	@	£2·20	per kg
100 g	Onions	@	£0·46	per kg
100 g	Shallots	@	£0·85	per kg
500 g	Mushrooms	@	£1·40	per kg
1 bott	White wine	@	£0·92	per bott
350 g	Butter	@	£1·35	per kg
3 dl	Cream	@	£1·15	per 1.
3	Eggs	@	£0·58	per doz
50 g	Parsley	@	£0·14	per kg

Prepare a dish costing sheet and show:
(a) The total food cost.
(b) The food cost per cover.
(c) The gross profit percentage gained if the dish is sold at £2·00 per cover.

2. The ingredients necessary for twelve portions of *Veal Stew* are as follows:

1·4 kg	Stewing veal	@	£2·59	per kg
200 g	Butter	@	£1·35	per kg
100 g	Flour	@	£0·20	per kg
700 g	Onions	@	£0·46	per kg
500 g	Mushrooms	@	£1·40	per kg
3	Eggs	@	£0·58	per doz
½	Loaf	@	£0·22	per loaf

	Bouquet garni	@	£0·05	
1·51	White veal stock	@	£0·04	per 1.
	Seasoning	@	£0·01	

Calculate:

(*a*) The food cost per portion.

(*b*) The selling price per portion necessary to produce a gross profit of 62% on sales.

3. The ingredients necessary to produce twelve portions of *Sole Colbert* are as follows:

12 × 400 g	Dover soles	@	£2·20	per kg
200 g	Butter	@	£1·35	per kg
300 g	Flour	@	£0·20	per kg
3	Eggs	@	£0·58	per doz
1	Loaf	@	£0·22	per loaf
4	Lemons	@	£0·08	each
5 1.	Frying oil (of which 10% is absorbed)	@	£0·60	per l.
1 sprig	Parsley	@	£0·04	per sprig

Find:

(*a*) The food cost per cover.

(*b*) The gross profit percentage on sales which will be achieved if the selling price is £2·20 per cover.

(*c*) What increase in selling price per cover would be necessary to produce a gross profit of 60% on sales?

4. The following ingredients are necessary to produce twelve portions of *Flan aux Pommes*:

300 g	Flour	@	£0·20	per kg
150 g	Margarine	@	£1·08	per kg
80 g	Sugar	@	£0·39	per kg
2	Eggs	@	£0·58	per doz
1·8 kg	Cooking apples	@	£0·40	per kg
1	Lemon	@	£0·08	each
200 g	Granulated sugar	@	£0·28	per kg
200 g	Apricot jam	@	£0·56	per kg

Find:

(*a*) The food cost per portion.

(*b*) The selling price per portion if a supplement of 140% on food cost is to be used.

5. The following ingredients are necessary to produce fifteen portions of *Crêpes au Citron*:

1 litre	Milk	@ £0·19	per 1.
400 g	Flour	@ £0·20	per kg
4	Eggs	@ £0·58	per doz
300 g	Castèr sugar	@ £0.39	per kg
4	Lemons	@ £0·08	each

Calculate:

(a) The cost per portion.

(b) The selling price per portion to produce a 60% gross profit.

(c) The increased selling price per portion to produce the same gross profit percentage if the cost of ingredients increases by £0·08 for fifteen portions.

6. (a) Explain why it is desirable to work to a fixed percentage of gross profit.

(b) On the luncheon menu of a refectory there were three items priced: A 66p; B 52p; C 39p. Assuming that the selling price is calculated on the basis of 45% gross profit, calculate the food cost of each item.

(H.C.I.M.A.)

7. One method of pricing food items on a menu is to fix their price by increasing the ingredient cost by a constant percentage. Do you consider this a good policy? Discuss, giving reasons for your opinion.

(H.C.I.M.A.)

8. Prepare a dish costing sheet for *Melon Frappé*, using the following ingredients for twenty-four covers, and show the food cost per cover: 4 melons, 100 g glacé cherries, 150 g caster sugar, 50 g ginger.

9. Prepare a dish costing sheet for *Steak and Kidney Pie*, using the following ingredients for twenty-four covers, and show the food cost per cover: 2·2 kg stewing steak, 700 g kidney, 550 g flour, 1·1 l. brown stock, 450 g onions, 50 g margarine, 300 g cooking fat; seasoning, etc., to be taken at 2p.

10. Prepare a dish costing sheet for *Crème Caramel* using the following ingredients for twenty-four covers, and show the ingredients cost per cover: 3·4 l. milk, 1½ doz large eggs, 100 g granulated sugar, 450 g lump sugar; use of vanilla sticks 1p.

11. Prepare a costing for 100 covers of *Coq au Vin Bourguignonne*, using the following ingredients:

25 × 1·2 kg Poulets	900 g Collar bacon
200 g Butter	450 g Shallots
2·7 kg Button onions	50 g Garlic
4 botts Red wine	1·5 dl Oil
9 l. Brown sauce	

    Show:
    (a) The food cost per cover.
    (b) The charge per cover to give a gross profit of 60%.

12. Prepare a costing sheet for four portions of *Cream of Tomato Soup*, and find the selling price necessary to produce a gross profit of 65% on sales. The ingredients necessary are as follows:

50 g Flour	100 g Carrots
50 g Tomato Purée	100 g Onions
50 g Butter	Bouquet garni, etc. (say 2p)
6 dl White stock	30 g Bacon trimmings

13. Use the following ingredients to prepare a dish costing sheet for four portions of *Lancashire Hotpot:*

550 g Stewing lamb	50 g Leeks
1·1 l. Brown stock	50 g Celery
450 g Potatoes	50 g Butter
100 g Onions	Seasoning, etc. (say 1p)

    (a) If the selling price is 52p per portion, what gross profit percentage is being achieved?
    (b) What alteration to the selling price would be necessary in order to achieve a.gross profit of 60%?

14. The following ingredients are required for four portions of *Fricassée of Veal:*

450 g Stewing veal	30 g Butter
30 g Flour	6 dl White stock
1 Egg yolk (½ egg)	1 dl Cream
200 g Button onions	200 g Button mushrooms
Seasoning and lemon juice (say 1p)	

    Find:
    (a) The food cost per cover.

(b) The selling price to give a gross profit of 58% if the cost of ingredients increases by £0·051 per portion.

15. The following ingredients are required for ten portions of *Navarin Printanier*:

50 g Clarified fat	900 g Button mushrooms
900 g Stewing lamb	900 g Potatoes
8 dl Brown stock	50 g Peas
30 g Flour	50 g French Beans
900 g Carrots	Parsley and a pinch of sugar
1·8 kg Turnips	(1p)

Find:

(a) The selling price to give a 63% gross profit.
(b) The selling price to give a 63% gross profit if the cost of stewing lamb increases to £1·20 per kg.

PRICE LIST

Bacon trimmings £0·08 kg	Kidney £1·10 kg
Brown sauce £0·06 l.	Leeks £0·56 kg
Brown stock £0·04 l.	Lump sugar £0·38 kg
Butter £1·35 kg	Margarine £1·08 kg
Button onions £0·59 kg	Melons £0·65 each
Button mushrooms £1.54 kg	Milk £0·19 l.
Carrots £0·49 kg	Oil £0·60 l.
Caster sugar £0·39 kg	Onions £0·46 kg
Celery £0·47 kg	Peas £0·52 kg
Clarified fat £0·54 kg	Potatoes £0·33 kg
Collar bacon £1·10 kg	Poulets £0·90 kg
Cooking fat £0·48 kg	Red wine £0·90 bott
Cream £1·15 l.	Shallots £0·85 kg
Eggs £0·58 doz	Stewing lamb £1·05 kg
Flour £0·20 kg	Stewing steak £1·85 kg
French beans £0·55 kg	Stewing veal £2·59 kg
Garlic £0·62 kg	Tomato purée £0·42 kg
Ginger £0·60 kg	Turnips £0·24 kg
Glacé cherries £1·94 kg	White stock £0·04 l.
Granulated sugar £0·28 kg	

4. *Banquets*

A BANQUET or special party costing in its simplest form may be very similar to a dish costing, the cost of food being ascertained, and the charge to the customer being calculated by reference to the required gross profit percentage. However, a banquet is a much larger unit of sales than a single dish, and it should therefore be possible to establish the actual costs to a much greater extent, leaving less to be estimated as a percentage of sales. Cost of additional labour and certain direct expenses such as menus, floral decorations, band hire, etc., can be estimated with reasonable accuracy.

General overheads and net profit, however, still need to be provided for on the basis of a percentage of sales. From our annual or monthly profit statements it can be established what percentage of total sales the general overheads amount to, and what is a reasonable net profit percentage. Similar proportions can then be allowed for in the charge for the banquet.

Example 1

Food cost   109.52
Labour   52.98   22½
O/hds   12½
net   162.50
total labour cost

In preparing a luncheon for 100 persons it is estimated that the total food cost will be £109·52, additional cost of staff will be £52·98, and overheads should be allowed for at 22½% of sales. What charge per cover should be made in order to produce a net profit of 12½%?

The answer to this problem lies in the basic understanding of the elements of sales dealt with in Chapter 2. Sales are made up of the total of food cost, labour cost, overheads, and net profit. So, in this example, the total charge for the luncheon will be the total of £109·52, £52·98, 22½% of sales, and 12½% of sales. Putting these facts together, we find that £162·50 plus 35% of sales equals the total charge, or 100% and £162·50 must therefore be 65% of the total charge. Once we know any item as both an amount and a percentage of sales, it is a simple matter to calculate the charge to be made. The amount should be divided by the percentage and multiplied by 100. Thus if £162·50 is 65%, then £162·50 divided by 65 $\dfrac{(£162·50)}{65}$ is 1%, and this multiplied

by 100, i.e. $$\frac{(£162·50 \times 100)}{65}$$ *for 100 hundred*
÷ again by 100

is 100% or total sales, in this case amounting to £250·00. This being the charge for 100 covers, the charge per cover will be this amount divided by 100, or £2·50.

The working for this is best set out as shown below, with each item having its amount, if known, and its percentage of sales, if known, entered side by side. Some amounts or percentages will not be known, and in those cases a space should be left for them to be entered when they have been worked out. This will be possible first with the percentages, if we remember that the percentages of all the elements of sales will together add up to 100% of sales.

Banquet for 100 persons

	£	Percentage of sales
Food cost	109·52	
Labour cost	52·98	
Overheads		22½
Net profit		12½

It will be seen that of the four items, we know the amount of two items, and the percentage of two items. The total of all four items is the charge to the customer, or total sales. We *do not know the amount* of this, but we *do know that the percentage* is 100%, since the percentage is based on sales, and the whole of anything must be 100% of it. So we can add in pencil the two percentages we are given, and find that they total 35%, and knowing that they and the other two items total 100%, we can see that the other two items total 65%. At this point we would add the amounts of food cost and labour cost in order to find out what amount is 65% of sales. All that remains is to divide this amount by 65 and multiply by 100 to find the total sales.

1) Express Labour cost as % sales ?
1) 52·98 ÷ 2·5 = 21·2%
1) 52·98 × 100 = 21·2%
*   250*

Example 2

The food cost for a banquet for 120 persons is costed at £2·70 per cover. Cigarettes and flowers are to be provided at a cost of £19·50, and a small band at a cost of £82·00. Additional labour cost will be £268·00, and general overheads should be provided for on the basis of 20% of sales. What charge per cover should be made in order to achieve a net profit of 10%?

Answer		£	%
	Total food cost (120 × £2·70)	324·00	
	Labour cost	268·00	
	Cigarettes and flowers	19·50	
	Band	82·00	
		693·50	70%
	General overheads	198·14	20%
	Net profit	99·07	10%
		£990·71	100%

Since all expenses and net profit together make up 100% of sales, and the unknown expenses and net profit add up to 30% of sales, the known expenses £693·50 must be 70% of sales.

From this the amount of sales can be calculated as

$$\frac{£693·50 \times 100}{70} = £990·71$$

or £8·256 per cover.

As a check the remaining figures can now be entered on the statement above. General overheads will be £198·14 (20% of £990·71). Net profit will be £99·07 (10% of £990·71). These amounts added to the total of other costs (£693·50) make up the total sales £990·71.

This example illustrates the basic principle, which can be adapted for various combinations of information which may be available or can be estimated. Having calculated the selling price in this way, however, it will be interesting to calculate the gross profit percentage being achieved and compare it with that expected from normal service. In this case the gross profit will be £666·71 (sales £990·71 less food cost £324·00) and the gross profit percentage is therefore 67·3%. This may be regarded as a high margin return, the term used to denote a rate of gross profit which is higher than the average. The term may apply to the restaurant generally (a luxury restaurant will usually need a high margin return in order to cover its higher overheads) or to one operation as in the case of this banquet.

The high margin return on this operation may be attributed to a combination of factors:

1. The food cost for a given number of covers may well be less

than normal because knowledge of how many meals will be served, and service within a short space of time, both contribute to reducing waste.

2. Labour cost and overheads may well be higher than normal as a result of giving better-than-usual service at a special luncheon. In this example labour cost is 23·0%, which may be normal, but total overheads amount to 34·3%, which may be regarded as high.

As a result of the above, the proportions of food cost and gross profit have changed. Net profit will be the normal proportion of sales, but the cost emphasis has moved from food to expenses.

It should not be thought, however, that this kind of operation will always necessitate a high margin return as a matter of course. In general terms, a special party outside normal service will incur abnormal expenses requiring a high margin return, while a party which can be fitted into normal service may, by utilizing existing expenses to the full, warrant a low margin return.

The question of management policy may enter into the decision as to what margin should be applied to a banquet. It may be desired to build up this kind of trade, and for this purpose to accept a low return, at least temporarily. On the other hand, it may be thought that this is the ultimate in luxury trade, from which a high return may be expected. In either case the return expected by the management, whether high or low, is the *net* return, or net profit after allowing for all expenses. The question of margin only arises from policy decisions in finding out what is necessary to cover the expenses and the required net profit.

Where the margin on a special operation is abnormal due to a change in cost emphasis, it should be ascertained whether the abnormality is tending towards a high margin return or a low margin return, and why. There may be perfectly good reasons for either effect, but in any particular case it should be clear that the valid reasons are having the expected effect. The following are possible reasons for a low margin return:

1. Food cost may be higher than normal due to inclusion of expensive dishes. If selling price is nevertheless calculated to produce a normal net profit percentage, and expenses are normal, then food cost will be an abnormally high percentage, and gross profit correspondingly low.

2. Concentration of service into a shorter time than would be necessary for chance custom may result in labour cost being low by comparison. The gross profit necessary to cover the labour cost would therefore be correspondingly lower.
3. The cost of such expenses as gas and electricity will not be so high for 100 covers served together as for the same number spread over a whole evening. The gross profit required will therefore be that much lower.
4. Purchasing pre-prepared food means that initial food cost is higher in order·to save on other costs in preparation, and the required gross profit will therefore be less.

EXERCISES

1. A banquet is to be prepared for 100 covers, and it is estimated that the following costs will be incurred: butcher £82·35; fishmonger £78·36; greengrocer £31·56; grocer £42·54; dairy £5·19; wages of extra staff £114·00; overheads £66·00. It is required to make a net profit of $12\frac{1}{2}\%$ of sales.
Calculate:
   (a) The charge to the customer per cover.
   (b) The rate of gross profit which will be made.
2. The following costs are estimated for a banquet of 100 covers: wages £133·05; butcher £69·54; greengrocer £17·85; dairy £6·72; fishmonger £49·23; stores issues £69·36; overheads £100·50.
   (a) Calculate what charge per cover should be made in order to achieve a net profit of 15%.
   (b) What rate of gross profit will be made?
   (c) Express the wages and overheads as a percentage of sales.
3. Food cost for a banquet of 100 covers is estimated to be £205·05 and labour cost £141·45. Overheads are to be allowed for at 20% of sales, and it is desired to make a net profit of 10%. Find the charge per cover which will be necessary.
4. A banquet of 140 covers is to be prepared for which the food cost will be £258·75 and labour cost will be £160·83. Overheads are to be allowed for at $17\frac{1}{2}\%$ of sales.
Find:
   (a) The charge per cover necessary to achieve a net profit of $12\frac{1}{2}\%$.

(b) The amount of net profit which will be made on the banquet.
5. The following are the costs of a banquet menu already approved
by the clients. You are asked to calculate: *(a)* total cost per cover;
(b) net profit per cover; *(c)* charge per cover; *(d)* gross profit per
cover; *(e)* food cost per cover.
Costs for 50 covers:

Food	£
Greengrocer	12·08
Stores	15·80
Fishmonger	21·28
Butcher	24·24
Dairy	2·56

Other costs	
Wages – extra staff	51·08
Proportion of fixed overheads (including permanent banqueting staff)	60·00

Note: It is required to achieve a net profit of 10% on sales.

(H.C.I.M.A.)

6. You are preparing your banqueting tariff brochure for the coming
season. You estimate the food cost for menu *A* for fifty covers will
be £85·28. Your staff and overhead charges for such a banquet
are estimated at £117·22.
  (a) Calculate the charge per cover to attain a net profit on sales of
  10%.
  (b) Calculate the estimated net profit from a banquet of fifty
  covers using this menu.
  (c) Calculate the cost of food percentage on sales.

(H.C.I.M.A.)

7. You have been given a menu for a banquet which you are required
to price for your general manager. Calculate the amount to be
charged by the Company on a per head basis and lay out your
facts and figures as you would present them to him.
  You are given the following information:
  The banquet is to take place at the Shorefore Hotel on 28
September 19... It is for the Beachcombers' Association. You
have calculated the food cost as £172·96. Wines are extra. Labour
cost is calculated as likely to be £202·04. There are 100 covers.

Overheads are reckoned at 15% on sales. Anticipated profit to be aimed for 10% on sales.

(H.C.I.M.A.)

8. You have been asked to arrange a special function for 120 persons for which the menu has been chosen. A small band is to be engaged for the occasion which will cost £45·00. Special menus are to be printed at a cost of £16·50, floral decorations will be required for the tables, and cigarettes are to be provided. Flowers and cigarettes cost £13·50. Labour cost is calculated at £129·00 and overheads are to be allowed for at 20% of sales. If the food cost of the chosen menu is £174·00, calculate:

   (a) What charge per cover should be quoted in order to achieve a net profit of 10%?

   (b) What will be the total amount of the bill if 10% is added for gratuities?

5. Meat Costing

THE costing of meat which is not purchased in pre-portioned form presents certain problems. First is the fact that while the portion to be served may be specified by weight, the *total* weight to be served is not the same as the total weight on which the purchase price is based. Sirloin of beef may cost £2·60 per kg, but it would be wrong to cost a 100 g portion of roast beef as one-tenth of £2·60, or £0·260. The true answer is likely to be twice as much because the commodity being served, roast beef, is not the commodity being purchased at £2·60 per kg, which was raw beef and bone. A change has taken place between purchase and serving, particularly a change in total weight, due to bones, trimming, and cooking shrinkage. The lost weight has been paid for, and is a cost of the meat served in addition to the quoted price per kilo.

Example

36 kg of beef are purchased at £1·85 per kg, the total cost being £66·60. After boning, trimming, cooking, and carving it is found that 240 90 g portions are obtained. The food cost of meat served is thus £0·278 per portion (£66·60 ÷ 240) or £3·083 per kg (240 × 90 g = 21·6 kg; £66·60 ÷ 21·6 = £3·083).

The calculation of the price of cooked meat may be expressed as a formula:

$$\text{cooked meat price per kg} = \frac{\text{raw meat price per kg} \times \text{raw meat weight}}{\text{cooked meat weight}}$$

cooked meat price per portion

$$= \frac{\text{raw meat price per kg} \times \text{raw meat weight}}{\text{number of portions}}$$

In this example the total weight was reduced from 36 kg of raw meat to 21·6 kg of served meat, and the price per kg increased from £1·85 per kg for raw meat to £3·083 per kg for served meat. It may be useful to express this information as a percentage formula for future use, deriving from the facts that 21·6 kg of cooked meat is 60% of

36 kg of raw meat, and a cooked meat price of £3·083 per kg is (100/60) × £1·85 per kg:

cooked meat price per kg

$$= \frac{\text{raw meat price per kg} \times 100}{\text{cooked meat percentage of raw meat}}$$

The amount of cooking shrinkage of roast meat will vary with the cooking temperature, the higher the temperature the more cooking loss, and leaving a joint for a time after cooking before carving will increase the number of portions it is possible to serve. This means that kitchen procedures need to be standardized before any hard and fast rules can be formulated, but some average weights of cooked meat expressed as a percentage of the raw weight are indicated below:

Joint	Cooking method	Cooked weight percentage of raw weight
Thin flank	Braised or stewed	35%
Flank	Braised or stewed	55%
Thick flank	Roasted	60%
Topside	Roasted	55%
Silverside	Boiled	55%
Rump	Roasted	50%
Sirloin	Roasted	50%
Wing end	Roasted	50%
Fore rib	Roasted	50%
Middle rib	Roasted	50%
Chuck rib	Roasted	50%
Brisket	Boiled	50%
Shin	Braised or stewed	55%

WHOLESALE CUTS

A further problem occurs when meat is bought in quantity and then butchered. There will be wastage in butchering, resulting in the price per kilo of usable meat being higher than the price per kilo actually paid. With careful weighing, this can be overcome, but the usable meat remaining will not all be one kind of meat, and should not all be priced the same.

The original cost must still be covered in allocating values to the usable meat, but where this includes any number of different cuts it is necessary to establish the price ratio between different cuts. The average price of usable meat may be £1·85 per kg, but it would be ridiculous to cost both sirloin and shank at the same price, because the sirloin has a greater relative value than the shank.

At this point we are not considering only the price of cooked meat for the purpose of costing a dish, but also the relative prices of raw meat purchased wholesale and then cut, or purchased pre-cut. The ultimate price of the cooked meat will be directly affected by the choice made between the two kinds of buying, and the decision will be affected by the relative cost.

As an example of the factors affecting this decision, a wholesale cut may be purchased, rump and loin XX costing £1·76 per kg, and comprising rump, sirloin, and fillet. The description XX indicates that the cut is without flank, suet, and kidneys. As an alternative, rump may be purchased pre-cut and ready for use at £3·50 per kg, sirloin at £2·60 per kg, and fillet at £4·40 per kg. For allocation of the cost to the different cuts in the rump and loin XX wholesale cut, it is convenient to use the same ratio as the retail prices.

If the rump and loin XX wholesale cut weighs 19 kg, the cost will be 19 × £1·76 = £33·44, and it may be found that after boning and trimming the result will consist of approximately the following:

	kg
Rump	3·5
Sirloin	6·0
Fillet	1·0
Stewing meat	4·0
Bones	4·0
Wastage	0·5
	19·0

The wastage is valueless, and bones may be priced at £0·10 per kg, value £0·40, which means that the meat cost is £33·04. Of this the stewing meat is incidental and may be valued at the market price £1·81 per kg, amounting to £7·24, which means that 10·5 kg of rump, sirloin, and fillet cost £25·80.

To allocate this wholesale cost to the different cuts in the same ratio as the retail prices the following formula should be used:

Wholesale price per kg

$$= \frac{\text{total wholesale cost}}{\text{total retail cost}} \times \text{retail price per kg}$$

If the total cost of meat purchased wholesale is £20, and the same meat would have cost £30 to buy retail, it can be seen that all the meat has cost 2/3rds of the retail price of that meat.

The total wholesale cost in the above example would be £25·80, being the total cost of the three cuts to be priced. The total retail cost would be as follows:

	£
Rump 3·5 kg @ £3·50 per kg =	12·25
Sirloin 6 kg @ £2·60 per kg =	15·60
Fillet 1 kg @ £4·40 per kg =	4·40
	32·25

The wholesale prices can now be calculated as follows:

$$\text{Rump} \quad \frac{£25·80}{£32·25} \times £3·50 \quad = \quad £2·80 \text{ per kg}$$

$$\text{Sirloin} \quad \frac{£25·80}{£32·25} \times £2·60 \quad = \quad £2·08 \text{ per kg}$$

$$\text{Fillet} \quad \frac{£25·80}{£32·25} \times £4·40 \quad = \quad £3·52 \text{ per kg}$$

If it is desired to calculate the cost of stewing meat as well, instead of treating it as an incidental at the market price, the same kind of calculation will be made using four items instead of three, using the total wholesale cost £33·04 instead of £25·80, and total retail cost £39·49 instead of £32·25. As the saving in cost will now be spread over four items instead of three, the principal cuts will be costed at a slightly higher price per kilo than before.

JOINTS

In dealing with the cost of joints purchased as wholesale cuts, the costing will be carried out in two stages. First the cost price per kilo of each joint must be established as described above, and adjustment will afterwards be made in respect of bone loss and cooking loss.

Example

A crop (wholesale cut) weighing 30 kg is purchased at £1·51 per kg, and is cut as follows:

	Weight with bone kg	Retail price
Fore rib	8	£2·50
Middle rib	7	£2·50
Chuck steak	7	£1·80
Chuck bone	3	£0·10
Leg of mutton cut	5	£1·98
	30	

Find the cost of a 100 g portion of roast beef using fore rib, and assuming a 50% bone and cooking loss.

Answer

The total wholesale cost of joints (excluding bones) is:

30 kg @ £1·51 per kg	=	£45·30
less 3 kg bones @ 10p per kg	=	0·30
		45·00

The total retail cost would be:

Fore rib	8 kg	@	£2·50 per kg	=	£20·00
Middle rib	7 kg	@	£2·50 per kg	=	17·50
Chuck steak	7 kg	@	£1·80 per kg	=	12·60
Leg of mutton cut 5 kg		@	£1·98 per kg	=	9·90
					60·00

$$\text{Cost of fore rib per kg} = \frac{£45·00}{£60·00} \times £2·50 = £1·875$$

$$\text{Cost of cooked meat after 50\% loss} = \frac{100}{50} \times £1·875 = £3·75$$

$$\text{Cost per portion} = \frac{100}{1000} \times £3·75 = £0·375$$

EXERCISES

1. (*a*) Explain what is meant by bone loss and cooking loss, and how they affect costing figures.

   (*b*) If bone loss and cooking loss together amount to 45% of the weight of raw meat costing £1·84 per kg, what is the cost per kilo of cooked meat?

2. Meat with bone is purchased at £1·70 per kg. Bone loss amounts to 15% of the total weight, and cooking loss is 30% of the boned weight. Calculate the cost per kilo of cooked meat.

3. A joint weighing 8·1 kg is purchased at £1·80 per kg. After cooking and carving it is found that fifty 90 g portions are obtained. Calculate:

   (*a*) The cost of a 90 g portion of served meat.

   (*b*) The cost per kilo of served meat.

4. A joint weighing 6·2 kg is purchased at £1·65 per kg. After cooking and carving it is found that thirty-eight 90 g portions are obtained. Calculate:

   (*a*) The cost of a 90 g portion of served meat.

   (*b*) The cost per kilo of served meat.

5. A joint weighing 7·2 kg is purchased at £1·55 per kg, and when boned produces 1·8 kg bones and 5·4 kg meat. Bones may be valued at 10p per kg. What is the cost per kilo of usable meat? What is the cost per kilo of served meat if cooking loss is 40%?

6. A wholesale cut weighing 17 kg is purchased at £1·80 per kg. After boning and trimming the result is 10 kg of steak meat, 3 kg of stewing meat, and 4 kg of bones. Bones are to be valued at 10p per kg, and stewing meat at £1·60 per kg. What is the cost per kilo of steak meat?

7. A wholesale cut weighing 18 kg costs £1·88 per kg and produces 10 kg of steak meat, 4 kg of stewing meat, and 4 kg of bones. The bones are valued at 10p per kg, and the steak meat and stewing meat are to be costed in proportion to their retail prices of £4·20 and £1·65 respectively. Find the wholesale cost of usable meat per kilo.

8. A wholesale cut weighing 25 kg costs £1·90 per kg, and produces 14 kg of steak meat, 6 kg of stewing meat, and 5 kg of bones valued at 10p per kg. The retail price of steak meat is £4·20

per kg, and stewing meat is £1·70 per kg. What is the wholesale cost per kilo of each type of meat?

9. A wholesale cut weighing 22 kg costs £1·95 per kg, and produces 13 kg of steak meat, 4 kg of stewing meat, and 4·5 kg of bones. The difference is wastage. If bones are taken at 10p per kg, what is the cost per kilo of each type of meat? The retail prices of steak meat and stewing meat are £4·25 and £1·70 respectively.

10. A wholesale cut weighing 20·2 kg costs £1·90 per kg. After cutting, it produces 3·5 kg of bones, 5 kg of stewing meat, and fifty-five 200 g steaks. The retail price of stewing meat is £1·70 per kg, and steak meat retails at £4·20 per kg. Bones are valued at 10p per kg. Find the cost of a 200 g steak.

(wholesale cut).
20.2 Kg costs £1·90 per Kg.

Bones 3.5 Kg   . 35p
                      8.50
Stewing meat 5.0 Kg
55 - 200g steaks £55·05   4 6·20   £38.38
Retail price g stewing meat is £1·70 per Kg
Steak meat retails at £4·20 per Kg
Bones 10p per Kg.

    Find the cost g a 200g steak?

Retail Price g Item   =   Item cost
   Total Retail   Total Cost g Item

    35   =   ¥   = 24p   -cost g
   55·05   38·38   bones

6. *Portion Control*

WHEN a customer in a sweet shop buys some sweets, he specifies what weight of sweets he wants, and the shopkeeper will carefully weigh them to see that he gives correct weight. By this means both customer and shopkeeper are satisfied that the correct value for money is given. The customer will continue to patronize the shop, and the shopkeeper will know that provided his costings are right, his return will be right, because he will know that the prices he has charged are correct for the quantities of goods he has sold.

The same accuracy in measuring quantities sold is expected in many other transactions. A litre of petrol purchased for £0·20 is expected to be one litre, no more, no less. The price has been fixed for that quantity, and if the quantity given for the price were to vary due to slackness, when multiplied by the millions of petrol sales the difference between expected sales and actual sales could be enormous. Similarly bars of chocolate are of uniform size, packets of detergent produced by the same manufacturer all contain the same quantity of detergent, jars of pickle will contain a specified number of grams of pickle.

In each case the manufacturer or supplier goes to some trouble to ensure that the quantity he sells for a given price is consistently the same quantity. The quantity will be the portion size he has used in his costings in calculating the selling price, and he will control this size to ensure that his costings are not invalidated. His method of controlling the size of each unit of sale is to use suitable equipment. For petrol sales special pumps are used which are capable of delivering carefully measured quantities. Other goods may be sold in containers large enough to contain only the right quantity, or if sold in a container that is larger than necessary, the quantity is measured by hand or by machine.

In catering, the reasons for portion control are just as strong, and the methods used will be very similar, in that suitable equipment will be used to regulate the size of portions of each commodity. Such equipment will include the following:

Scales
Slicing machines
Measuring jugs
Graded scoops and ladles
Standard-size baking tins
Standard-size cups, glasses, soup bowls
Bar optics
Pre-packed portions

It may be argued that the last is not equipment, but the most positive portion control of all is to buy food already made up into the portion which is to be served.

It is noticeable that the largest and financially most successful catering establishments all employ highly developed portion control methods, and in some cases have done so for many years. Particularly with popular catering on low margins, it would be disastrous to leave food consumption to chance. As an example, the treatment of meat in the 1930s had already been organized to this degree:

1. A joint was weighed before and after cooking, and the cooking loss checked.
2. It was again weighed immediately before carving, to establish the responsibility of the carver.
3. When carving was finished, the bones and scrap were weighed, and the weight deducted from the total weight before carving.
4. The carver was held responsible for the number of portions equal to the net weight.

Scales should be available to check the weight of portions carved, but with practice a carver can estimate by eye alone a portion of given size with remarkable accuracy, provided a check is made with the scales occasionally to avoid gradual drifting away from the correct size.

Vegetables will be served with a scoop of a size to give just the weight already decided upon. A flan will be made in a tin of a size to give exactly six portions or exactly eight portions, so that there is never any doubt about how many customers will be served from a given quantity produced.

With all the proper equipment, however, portion control will not be successful without three things:

1. *Standard recipes* – the article produced must consist of the same ingredients every time, or the portions cannot be consistent even

if they are the same weight. This particularly applies to garnishes. Including an expensive garnish on impulse can ruin the cost of a dish.

2. *Portion charts* – if staff are to serve the correct portions they must know what those portions are. Charts showing this should be displayed at convenient points in the kitchen for ready reference. The way in which the portion size is expressed should be convenient to the server. A portion may be thought of as 50 g for costing purposes, but to the server becomes '1 × No. 2 scoop'.

3. *Regular checking* – supervision must be so automatic that there is no thought of varying the system. In this way correct habits are developed and need no special effort.

It should be emphasized that the expression 'portion control' means just what it says, the control of portion size to ensure that portions served are consistently the same size as the portions costed. It *does not mean* limitation of portion size so that portions are small. The actual size of portions may be large or small, and is a matter of policy to be decided by the management. Portion control is used to ensure that the decision once made is adhered to consistently.

EXERCISES

1. Explain what is meant by portion control, and why it is necessary.
2. What costing advantages may be expected from using pre-portioned foods?
3. Why is it important to use standard recipes? How would you ensure that the standard recipe is followed every time?
4. Write short explanatory notes on
   (a) Elements of cost.
   (b) Portion control.
   (c) Treatment of staff meals.
   (H.C.I.M.A.)
5. *(a)* Explain what is meant by portion control.
   (b) Comment on the importance of portion control as a method of food cost control.
   (c) Give six examples of portion control equipment.
   (H.C.I.M.A.)
6. List four examples of portion control equipment, and state briefly

in each case how the control is effected by using such a piece of equipment.

(H.C.I.M.A.)

7. What is the purpose of portion control? How is it achieved?

(H.C.I.M.A.)

8. Portion control equipment is used in the kitchen, the restaurant, and the bar. Give two examples of equipment used in each department.

7. Food Control and Takings Control

EFFICIENT control of food purchases entails some system and method being used to record the coming and going of goods, and the amount of stock in hand. Without such a control losses are inevitable, due to unnoticed waste, pilfering, or just bad buying. This is not to suggest that the business will necessarily make an overall loss, although this may happen, but a loss will be incurred in the sense that profits will not be as high as they should be.

It should be emphasized at once that the quantity of records necessary to achieve the required control will vary according to the nature of the business. A small business with a high degree of personal supervision by the proprietor, and keeping small stocks, will need very little in the way of stores records. At the other extreme, a business with a central stores supplying several branches, buying in bulk, and carrying large stocks, will need very detailed records indeed. The decision on what records are necessary in any particular case will depend on one factor only. Is the person with the ultimate responsibility able to account for the usage of all goods purchased? If so, adequate records are kept. If not, then something further is needed.

Purchasing

A written record of items ordered is provided by an *order book*, printed in duplicate so that a carbon copy is retained in the book. If this is completed for *every* order, including those given by telephone, a complete record of orders is available for subsequent checking with delivery notes and invoices. Among other uses it is a safeguard against misunderstanding with a supplier as to whether an order was for 5 or 5 dozen!

Goods Received

When goods are received the quantities should be checked and entered in a *goods received book* (Figure 3). Quality may be checked immedi-

Goods received				
Date	Supplier	Qty.	Description	Order No.

Figure 3. Goods received book

ately, or may be checked later in the kitchen, and any complaints notified to the supplier, but it is essential that quantities should be checked immediately. In this connection care should be taken whether quantities are expressed in cases or dozens, and whether cases are inners or outers. It is essential to avoid confusion in the records by using an unambiguous description, even though the delivery note may be expressed differently. Thus '6 cases of A 2½ fruit cocktail' shown on the delivery note would be entered in the goods received book as '6 cases × 2 dozen tins A 2½ fruit cocktail'.

The column for order number can be completed subsequently

when convenient. Entering the order number ensures that it is confirmed that the goods *were* ordered, and not delivered in error. It also provides an opportunity for marking the carbon copy in the order book to show that the goods have been received, and this enables the buyer to chase up orders which have not yet been delivered. The *delivery note* is a convenient means of providing the cross-reference between goods received book and order book. After the goods have been checked and entered in the goods received book, the delivery note should be initialled and endorsed with the date of receipt of the goods. It should then be passed to the buyer for checking with the order, and when this has been done, the order number should be noted on the delivery note for return to the storeman, who will then enter the order number in the goods received book.

Bin Cards

Bin cards originated in engineering concerns where small components were kept in bins, and a card attached to each bin showed a running record of the quantity remaining in the bin. They are equally suitable for catering stocks, and the method is to enter on the cards the quantities of goods received and issued, and the balance remaining (Figure 4). The card should show the unit of quantity which is being used (kg, dozen, tins, etc.) and this should be the smallest unit likely to be issued. It is no use expressing quantities in dozens if issues are not

Unit_____					Item_____				
Date	Details	Received	Issued	Balance	Date	Details	Received	Issued	Balance

Figure 4. A bin card

Card x System - more sophisticated system.

always made in dozens. The result would be that entries on the bin card would be fractions, casing difficulty and the risk of error. It is much better to enter the quantities as single items, if the commodity will be issued that way, so that whole numbers are used.

Periodically a check should be made that the balance remaining according to the card agrees with the actual number of articles in store.

Stores Ledger

A _stores ledger_ can be likened to a collection of bin cards kept all together instead of spread around the store. It may be kept instead of, or as well as, the bin cards, and the ruling will be very similar, with the addition of some information regarding re-ordering of goods. It is essential that orders are placed soon enough before stocks run out, so that new deliveries will be received in time, and this means keeping a _minimum stock_. If issues of tinned orange juice average three tins per week, and deliveries take ten days from receipt of the order, then orders must be given when there are still five or six tins in stock. In this case it might be thought prudent to keep a minimum stock of six tins, and this would be marked on the ledger sheet for tinned orange juice. When an issue is being entered in the stores ledger which reduces the stock remaining to the minimum noted, an order is made out for replacements. It is often the practice to clip a coloured tag on to the page of the ledger to indicate items which are down to the minimum stocks.

To facilitate re-ordering it is useful also to keep a note on the ledger of _maximum stock_. This is the maximum quantity which the management consider may be held without unduly tying up liquid capital in stocks, and it provides a guide to the quantity which may be ordered. In deciding minimum and maximum stock quantities it will be necessary to consider the time taken by suppliers to deliver and the rate at which the item is used up. Weekly deliveries will normally call for a minimum stock equivalent to one week's consumption, and a maximum stock equivalent to two weeks' consumption.

Stores Issues

The goods used by the kitchen will include direct purchases of perishable goods, and withdrawals from store of other goods. The items purchased direct for the kitchen will be shown on invoices and totals can be derived from these, but withdrawals from store should be recorded on a *stores requisition* (*see* Figure 5). As its name implies

Qty	Description	Unit price	£
	Stores requisition	No.___	
Dept. _____		Date _____	

Figure 5. A stores requisition

this is primarily an order to the store to issue the goods listed on it, but the addition of a column for values provides a convenient source of information regarding the cost of transfers from stores to kitchen. Alternatively a *transfer note* may be used, which is a similar form suitable for recording the transfer of goods between any two departments in the same organization. The effect of both forms is to act as internal invoices.

Quantities issued will be noted from the stores requisition on to the appropriate bin cards and stores ledger accounts. When the values have been entered on the forms, these should be listed and the totals entered in the cost records. In preparing costing figures of the kitchen for a period of, say, a month, the amount included as 'purchases' will then be the total of direct purchases and stores issues.

STOCKS

The expression *stock-in-trade* is a general term relating to those goods which are bought and sold by a business with a view to making a profit. However, the records of purchases of stock-in-trade are usually referred to briefly as 'purchases', sales of stock-in-trade are referred to as 'sales', and the term 'stock' (or 'stock-in-hand') is used to mean the value of stock-in-trade held at a particular moment.

To ascertain the value of stock-in-hand it is first necessary to list on a *stock sheet* the quantities of each item held (Figure 6). The cost price per unit can then be entered from invoices or price lists, and the

	Stock in hand	Date_____		
	Dept._____			
Qty	Description		Unit price	Value

Figure 6. A stock sheet

values calculated. It is a fundamental principle of profit calculations that stock-in-hand shall be valued no higher than original cost. If the present value is less than original cost, then the lower value should be taken. The reason is that any profit-making there may be on the goods occurs only when they are sold. Any apparent increase in value of goods still held in stock should be disregarded until they are sold, since the value may well fall again before they are sold. This question will not arise with goods such as perishables which are used quickly, but may be of great importance in the case of goods which are kept for a considerable length of time. For example, bottled wine bought in quantity to mature on the premises may well be worth considerably more than it originally cost, and the increase in value will be taken account of when it is sold.

When goods are bought in quantity at intervals, and prices change, it is sometimes difficult to be certain of the original cost of issues or stock-in-hand. The particular goods may have been bought at the beginning of the year at £2·94 per dozen, half-way through the year at £3·00 per dozen, or at the end of the year at £3·25 per dozen, and unless the purchases at one price greatly outweighed the others it would be difficult to decide which price to use. In such cases there are two main methods in common use, known as LIFO (Last In, First Out) and FIFO (First In, First Out). The former assumes that issues will be from the latest purchases and priced accordingly, stocks remaining being priced at the earlier prices. FIFO, on the other hand, assumes that issues are from the earliest remaining purchases.

System of stock pricing not stock taking

Example

During the quarter ended 31 October 19.., purchases and issues of 822 g canned fruit cocktail were as follows:

	Purchased	*Issued*
August	36 @ £0·38 each = £13·68	30
September	30 @ £0·40 each = £12·00	26
October	24 @ £0·42 each = £10·08	25
	£35·76	

LIFO Method   £

August issues	30 @ £0·38 each		11·40
Stock remaining	6 @ £0·38 each		
September issues	26 @ £0·40 each		10·40
Stock remaining	6 @ £0·38 each		
	4 @ £0·40 each		
October issues	24 @ £0·42 each	£10·08	
	1 @ £0·40 each	£0·40	
		———	10·48
Stock remaining	3 @ £0·40 each	£1·20	
	6 @ £0·38 each	£2·28	
		———	3·48
			£35·76

FIFO Method   £

August issues	30 @ £0·38 each		11·40
Stock remaining	6 @ £0·38 each		
September issues	6 @ £0·38 each	£2·28	
	20 @ £0·40 each	£8·00	
		———	10·28
Stock remaining	10 @ £0·40 each		
October issues	10 @ £0·40 each	£4·00	
	15 @ £0·42 each	£6·30	
		———	10·30
Stock remaining	9 @ £0·42 each		3·78
			£35·76

Other Methods

Other methods of valuing issues of stock include the *average cost method* and the *replacement cost method*. The former depends on finding the new average cost of stock held when each new purchase is made. Issues are valued at this average cost until a new purchase necessitates a new average calculation. The replacement cost method is an extension to LIFO in that issues are valued at the price which would be paid to replace them, whether any goods have already been bought at that price or not.

These are not by any means the only methods in use, but whatever method is used it should be used consistently.

RESTAURANT AND HOTEL TAKINGS

Control of takings entails ensuring that customers are properly charged for goods and services supplied to them, and that payments by the customers are received in full and properly accounted for.

In the restaurant the method which is most simple and at the same time most successful is the *triplicate checking system*. Under this system a waiter's check book is used, having numbered checks in triplicate.

1. Each book has an identifying number, and each check within the book is consecutively numbered. The numbering provides a means of controlling the checks, so it is important that no check should be destroyed.
2. On each check the waiter writes the table number, room number (if applicable), the number of covers, the date, and his initials, in addition to the customer's order.
3. The top copy of the check is taken to the kitchen where it is used to order the meal.

    The second copy is taken to the cashier, who uses it to prepare the customer's bill. As each duplicate check is handed in, the price is added to the appropriate bill, so that bills are constantly kept up to date and will be readily available when called for.

    The third copy of the check is retained in the waiter's book for reference and will not be used unless some query arises.
4. The cashier's bills are made out in duplicate and show the same information as the waiters' checks. The top copy is used as the customer's receipt if the bill is paid, or as a charging copy for residents, and from the duplicate copy the cashier writes up a dissection sheet, showing the analysis of takings into food, wines, etc., and whether the bill has been paid or is to be charged.
5. After the meal, the total cash received, as recorded in the restaurant dissection sheet, is then paid in to the main cashier, or direct to the bank.
6. All top copies of waiters' checks are collected from the kitchen and taken to the control office, together with all second copies

from the cashier, the duplicate paid bills, and the dissection sheet. Charged bills are sent to reception for entering on the tabular ledger, and then to control office. In the control office all the records are checked against each other to ensure that everything has been charged, and that pricing is correct.

A similar check system may be used for other items charged by a hotel. Books of checks in duplicate or triplicate may be held by all the following staff to ensure that accurate charges are promptly recorded:

Chambermaids	*for*	morning teas
Housekeepers		laundry
Floor service		room service
Porter		newspapers and taxis
Garage attendant		garage
Telephonist		telephone calls
Bar		drinks

In each case one copy is sent to reception to be charged in the tab., and another copy or the book of check counterfoils will go to control office for checking.

EXERCISES

1. Describe briefly how a bin card system operates, and state its advantages and disadvantages.

(H.C.I.M.A.)

2. *(a)* Describe how you would check the incoming foodstuffs in a medium-sized hotel.
   (b) Give examples of any records/documents that might be used in connection with the checking of such foodstuffs.

(H.C.I.M.A.)

3. Draw up instructions for a newly appointed person to follow when checking incoming foodstuffs into a catering establishment. Illustrate your answer with any records or documents that such a person may see or use when carrying out his duties.

(H.C.I.M.A.)

4. Explain how the lack of regular checking of delivery notes can adversely affect the gross profit of an hotel.

5. Illustrate a bin card for tinned peach slices, size A $2\frac{1}{2}$, showing maximum stock 4 doz, minimum stock $\frac{1}{2}$ doz, stock at 1st June

14 tins, issued 3rd June 3 tins, issued 18th June 4 tins, received 20th June 24 tins, issued 27th June 3 tins.

6. Explain the use of a goods received book and illustrate a suitable ruling.
7. What is the purpose of a stores requisition? Explain what entries in other records will be made from a stores requisition note.
8. *(a)* When is a stores transfer note used?
   (b) What is meant by LIFO and FIFO?
9. At what price should stocks be valued? What value should be used on stock sheets, if stocks include goods bought at different prices?

8. Monthly Figures – Food Cost and Gross Profit

HAVING carefully calculated the costings for dishes to be sold and banquets to be given, it remains to be seen whether actual operations over a period of time have come up to expectations. A calendar month, or accounting period of four or five weeks, is a convenient length of time for which to prepare a statement of costs actually incurred, and the first information required would be the food cost during the period compared with the takings for the period.

We have already seen that if we take the food cost away from the takings, what is left is gross profit, and this can be expressed as a percentage of takings. We will already know roughly what we expect this percentage to be in order to cover other expenses and net profit, and will have based our dish costings on it. The different calculations are complementary, and each will be considered in the light of the other until a proper balance is achieved. The calculation of the food cost for the month, however, will not be arrived at in the same way as for a dish, when it was just a question of listing ingredients. In a restaurant it is not possible to list the ingredients of all the meals prepared in a month, so the total must be determined by reference to the total value of food purchased during the month and by finding out how much of this we have used. This can be done by deducting what is left at the end of the month from the total amount of food we have had during the month. This amount left at the end of the month, called 'stock-in-hand', is found by listing all food remaining in the kitchen and stores, and valuing it at *cost price*. If this is done at the end of every month, it follows that every month we shall begin operations with some stock already in hand *(opening stock)*, and will end the month with a different value of stock which is remaining at that date *(closing stock)*. The closing stock of one month is the opening stock of the next month.

Having added all our purchases of food for the month, the total should be added to the value of opening stock, and from this total the closing stock should be deducted. The result is the cost of food used:

food cost = opening stock + purchases — closing stock

Example

The net purchases of food during the month of June amounted to £875, the value of stock on 1 June being £115 and on 30 June £168. What was the cost of food consumed during the month?

Answer

		£
Opening stock		115
Purchases		875
		990
Less Closing stock		168
Cost of food consumed		£822

The total of purchases should be the *net* total after deducting any returns or allowances. This should be borne in mind particularly when goods have been returned just before the end of the month, and the credit note has not yet been received. In this case allowance must be made for the credit note which has still to come, or the purchases will be overstated.

Example

From the following information calculate the amount of gross profit for the month of August and express the gross profit as a percentage of sales: purchases £1,347; sales £3,393; stock at 1 August £156; stock at 31 August £130; purchases returns £16.

Answer

		£
Sales		3,393
Food cost:		
Opening stock		156
Purchases	1,347	
Less Returns	16	1,331
		1,487
Less Closing stock		130
		1,357
Gross profit		£2,036

Gross profit percentage:

$$\frac{2,036 \times 100}{3,393} = 60 \cdot 0\%$$

TABULAR GROSS PROFIT STATEMENTS

We have seen in Chapter 3 that not all items of output will necessarily be priced to give the same gross profit percentage. For a given volume of sales it will be known what overall percentage is needed to cover labour cost, overheads, and net profit, but this may be achieved by pricing some items to give a higher percentage and some to give a lower percentage. Analysis of the sales mix is important in this connection if the effect of the varying percentages on the total is to be foreseen, and it will be necessary to check the effect by preparing a *tabular gross profit statement* to show the gross profit achieved on each category of sales.

Example

A restaurant has a turnover in June of £3,000, and at this level of sales it is necessary to make a gross profit of 61 % of sales. Sales are divided into three main types: meals, fruit, and sundries (the latter being ready-to-serve foods such as bread rolls, butter pats in pre-packed portions, etc.). Menu prices have been fixed to give different gross profit percentages on the different types of sales. From the following information prepare a tabular gross profit statement to show the gross profit percentage achieved for the month in total and for each category.

		£
Stock at 1 June	Fresh fruit	2
	Sundries	11
	Other foodstuffs	82
Stock at 30 June	Fresh fruit	4
	Sundries	9
	Other foodstuffs	102
Purchases during June	Fresh fruit	92
	Sundries	193
	Other foodstuffs	900
Sales during June	Fresh fruit	200
	Sundries	400
	Meals	2,400

GROSS PROFIT STATEMENT FOR JUNE

	Total £	Fruit £	Sundries £	Meals £
Sales	3,000	200	400	2,400
Food cost:				
Stock at 1 June	95	2	11	82
Purchases	1,185	92	193	900
	1,280	94	204	982
Less Stock at 30 June	115	4	9	102
	1,165	90	195	880
Gross Profit	1,835	110	205	1,520
Gross profit %	61·1%	55·0%	51·2%	63·3%

It will be seen that with this sales mix a gross profit percentage of 63·3% on meals, 51·2% on sundries, and 55% on fruit produced an overall gross profit of 61·1% for the month. If the sales mix had been in different proportions the overall result would have been different.

An example showing an extreme change in sales mix will demonstrate this more clearly:

Total sales £3,000, as above, made up of fruit £2,400, sundries £400, meals £200.

	Sales	*G.P.%*	*Gross profit*
Fruit	£2,400	55·0%	£1,320
Sundries	400	51·2%	205
Meals	200	63·3%	127
	3,000		1,652 = 55·1%

STAFF MEALS

One perquisite of most employees in hotels and restaurants consists of free meals supplied by the employer. The wages paid are fixed in the knowledge that staff will be supplied with meals, and the value of such meals is just as much a cost of employing staff as the amount of wages paid in cash. We shall consider in Chapter 10 how many things may need to be taken into account to arrive at the true cost of employing staff, but the question of staff meals has another aspect, since it directly affects the calculation of gross profit.

If meals are supplied to staff, it follows that not all the food has been supplied to customers. In calculating gross profit it is necessary to deduct from sales the cost of food sold, which means the cost of food supplied to customers, but when the amount of food purchases is adjusted to allow for stocks, the result is the cost of food used for both sales and staff meals. If this total food cost is deducted from food sales the resultant figure will appear to give a very low gross profit percentage. Out of season the result may even appear to be a gross loss.

The reason is that the difference between food sales and total food cost is not gross profit, but gross profit less that part of labour cost paid in meals. What proportion of sales this is will vary according to season, and in a holiday town just after Easter, the staff may out-number the customers, with the result that total food cost is greater than food sales. A few weeks later the situation will have radically changed, and it will appear that a gross loss has been turned into a gross profit, when in fact the relationship between sales and cost of sales has really remained the same.

The danger in this situation is that the uncertainty as to the true gross profit percentage caused by the distortion of staff meals can lead to acceptance of a lower percentage as due to this cause, when in fact there is another cause which should be remedied.

For this reason it is important to adjust the costing figures by deducting the value of staff meals from food cost, and adding it to labour cost. It is not sufficient just to deduct the amount from one place and then forget it. The cost has been incurred and must be taken into account. It is just a case of starting out under the wrong description from a cost point of view, so it must be taken from one place and put back in another place, the other place being *labour cost*.

The method of valuing staff meals will usually entail costing the food supplied to a member of staff in one day. This can be done several times until a fair average is found, which may be, for example, £0·40 per day. If eight staff are employed, each eating in for six days each week, then the cost of staff meals for a four-week period would be:

$$8 \text{ (staff)} \times 24 \text{ (days)} \times £0.40 = £76.80$$

This amount, £76·80, should be *deducted from food cost and added to labour cost*.

If some staff have meals on more days than others, or if some have meals of a greater value than others, the calculation should be adjusted accordingly:

3 staff eat in for 7 days per week (cost £0·50 per day)
4 staff eat in for 6 days per week (cost £0·50 per day)
5 part-time staff for 6 days per week (cost £0·25 per day)

Value of staff meals for 4 weeks:

$$3 \times 28 \times £0.50 = £42.00$$
$$4 \times 24 \times £0.50 = £48.00$$
$$5 \times 24 \times £0.25 = £30.00$$

Total value of staff meals £120·00

Care should be taken in assuming that part-time staff meals will be one-half the cost of meals taken by full-time staff. It has been assumed so in the above example for purposes of illustration, and it will sometimes be true in practice, but more often than not the cost of meals for part-time staff will be more than half the full-time rate. Whether the difference will have any material effect will depend on the numbers involved.

If there are many staff, and the calculation of staff meals is complicated by the incidence of split duties, part-time work, or different cost of meals for different grades of staff, it will be found easier if the meals are valued by the wages clerk on the time-sheet of each employee. At this time when the time-sheets are being examined for payroll purposes, the extra question of what meals would have been taken each day does not involve a lot of additional trouble. Afterwards it is a simple matter to add-list the weekly values of staff meals shown on all the time-sheets. To this total must be added the cost of meals taken by managerial and any other salaried staff who do not appear on time-sheets.

SOME PRACTICAL POINTS

A restaurant or hotel will probably find that its monthly figures of purchases and sales are rather more complicated than the above illustrations. The importance of achieving the hoped-for percentage is so great that instead of waiting until postings to the ledger have been completed, it is customary to collect the figures from the subsidiary books as soon as they have been totalled. This means that each item in the calculation of gross profit may be made up of several amounts from different sources, and care is needed to avoid overlooking a possible source. In view of the fact that this information will be wanted regularly every month, it may be useful to have a standard form duplicated which will simplify the calculation of gross profit and act as a reminder of the sources of information.

In Figure 7 it is assumed that the business is an hotel, and that meals taken by resident guests are recorded in columns of the tabular ledger, or tab., chance meals appear in the restaurant cash received book, and there are some parties and banquets which are invoiced and recorded in a sales day book. Once again the layout of the form should be adapted to suit the facts of the particular business concerned. The illustration assumes five headings in the tab. for food sales, but individual hotels may have more or less than this. Similarly, chance

Food gross profit		May 19_ _
	£	£
Takings		
Tabular ledger:		
Meals	5,870	
Morning coffee	18	
Lunch	62	
Afternoon tea	26	
Dinner	150	6,126
Cash received book		284
Sales day book		47
		6,457
Food cost		
Opening stock		146
Purchases:		
Purchases day book	2,325	
Petty cash book	23	
May accounts not yet entered	18	
	2,366	
Less April accounts included	29	2,337
Stores issues		356
		2,839
Deduct:		
Staff meals	184	
Closing stock	121	305
		2,534
Gross profit		3,923
Gross profit %		60·8 %

Figure 7.

meals may be recorded in the tab., in which case the gross profit
calculation will be drawn up accordingly.

Opening stock is the cost value of the kitchen stocktaking at the
end of the previous month, which is therefore the value of the food
with which we started this month. In this illustration it is assumed
that there is a stores separate from the kitchen, and that transfers
from stores to kitchen are separately recorded. Accordingly the value
of the stock in the stores would be ignored in this calculation.

Purchases should be the total of all purchases of food going
directly to the kitchen. Purchases for the stores should be excluded
since these will appear in the 'stores issues' figure when they eventually

go to the kitchen. The figure of purchases which is required is the total cost of goods delivered to the kitchen during the month, but it will usually happen that some invoices have not arrived by the time the gross profit calculation is required. In this case an addition will be required for the value of such accounts, and since the same thing probably happened last month, a deduction of last month's figure which will now be included in the day book for this month. Just as it is important to ensure that we include all the purchases for this month, so we must exclude any purchases which do not relate to this month.

Stores issues are, to the kitchen, merely purchases of the month which have come from within the hotel instead of from an outside supplier. Again care must be taken to include all issues during the month and nothing else.

Having entered all the food obtained by the kitchen during the month, it is necessary to deduct the value of the food not served to customers, i.e. staff meals and closing stock. When these amounts have been deducted, the remainder is the cost of food sold. This should now be deducted from total food takings to arrive at the gross profit, which is finally expressed as a percentage of takings.

EXERCISES

1. The gross purchases of a restaurant for the year amounted to £16,471, and returns amounted to £57. Stock-in-hand at 1 January was valued at £135 and at 31 December amounted to £163. Calculate the cost of food used in the year.
2. Calculate the cost of food used in the month of June if the opening stock was £87, closing stock was £93, and net purchases for the month amounted to £1,487.
3. The stock of food on hand at 1 April amounted to £176, gross purchases for the month were £1,819, goods costing £14 were returned, and the stock of food at 30 April was valued at £180. What was the cost of food used?
4. The Elite Restaurant employs seven staff who receive free meals for six days per week, the cost of meals taken by each member of staff being estimated at £0·50 per day.
   (a) Calculate the cost of staff meals for February.
   (b) Explain what adjustment should be made to the monthly cost figures in respect of staff meals.

5. The stock sheets of a restaurant showed that the total stock at 1 May amounted to £128. At 31 May the stock was £146. Net purchases amounted to £1,635 for the month, but adjustment is required in respect of staff meals estimated to cost £57 for the month. Prepare a statement showing the cost of food sold for the month.

6. From the following figures prepare a statement to show the cost of food sold in the month of July:

Purchases during July	£1,811
Stock of food at 1 July	74
Stock of food at 31 July	98
Cost of staff meals for July	63

7. The following information was extracted from the books of the Popular Restaurant for the month of August:

Sales	£2,760
Purchases	1,172
Stock at 1 August	96
Stock at 31 August	115
Cost of staff meals for the month	59

Prepare a statement showing:
(a) The cost of food sold.
(b) The gross profit.
(c) The gross profit percentage of sales.

8. From the following information calculate the gross profit and the gross profit percentage of sales:

Sales	£2,280
Kitchen stock at 1 July	74
Kitchen purchases for July	582
Stores issues for July	261
Kitchen stock at 31 July	61
Staff meals for July	58

9. Write short notes on the importance of food cost control, and describe at least three different ways in which it is possible to control the cost of food used and maintain it at a predetermined percentage in relation to sales.

(H.C.I.M.A.)

10. *(a)* What is the purpose of a food costing system?

(*b*) The following information was extracted from the records of a restaurant in respect of April 19..:

Stock valuation on 1 April

	£
Meat	215·30
Vegetables	188·90
Sweets	46·70
Other foods	283·20

Stock valuation on 30 April (after business)

	£
Meat	163·40
Vegetables	212·10
Sweets	30·60
Other foods	201·80

Net purchases for April 19..

	£
Meat	355·60
Vegetables	443·20
Sweets	85·10
Other foods	134·40

Value of sales during April 19..

	£
Meat	968·70
Vegetables	1200·00
Sweets	303·70
Other foods	647·50

Prepare a statement in tabular form showing the amount of gross profit percentage of food on sales for the restaurant for the month in total and for each category.

(H.C.I.M.A.)

11. How are staff meals treated in the books of a catering concern?

(H.C.I.M.A.)

12. In a catering establishment during the month of March 19.. there had been credit purchases of food amounting to £1,720. Cash purchases of food were £332, and purchase returns £72 in the same period.

The stock of food on 1 March was £352.

The stock of food after business on 31 March was £388.

Sales during the month amounted to £3,600.

The expected gross profit on sales is 52%.

(a) Show in tabular form the value of food consumed.

(b) Calculate the actual percentage gross profit obtained, and the amount in sterling by which this differed from the anticipated profit.

(c) State briefly three reasons which might be the cause of such a difference.

(H.C.I.M.A.)

9. Wines and Spirits

THE gross profit expected from sales of wines and spirits will be lower than from sales of meals, because the costs to be met out of it are not so high. There will still be labour costs and a proportion of overheads which are attributable to this source of income, but the kitchen cost of meals will be missing.

As always, the gross profit must be sufficient to cover labour cost, overheads, and net profit, but if costs are proportionately lower while net profit is proportionately the same, then gross profit will be proportionately lower. In general the gross profit required on restaurant sales of drinks will be 50% of takings, which means that the pricing policy is a simple matter of adding 100% to cost, or doubling it.

As with food, however, this simple rule of thumb may be inadequate in some circumstances, or for certain items. What appears to be a reasonable pricing policy for most table wines may be varied for expensive items like champagne, and beer may be priced differently again.

CONTROL

The control of bar stocks is an important matter to a catering business, and if not properly handled can become a headache. The nature of the commodity is such, that any slackness in control presents an intolerable temptation to those who have access to the stock, so that losses may occur which will be difficult to detect and prevent. If to this is added a mixing of bar sales or purchases with food sales or purchases, the calculation of profit or loss on both operations will be misleading from the start. Yet bar stocks have one big advantage from a control point of view, the bottle is an easily counted unit for which a standard price is charged. This is important because it enables a check to be kept on the coming and going of stock by valuing all figures of stocks and purchases at selling price. The actual receipts from sales being already at 'selling price', the figures can then be reconciled, which may not be possible in any other way.

Reconciliation of stocks, by whatever method, means ensuring that sales account for the difference between the total of goods available during a period and the total of stock-in-hand at the end of the period, the total available during the period being the sum of the stock at the beginning plus the goods purchased during the period. This *may* be possible by reference to quantities:

Stock in hand on 1 June	184 bottles
Purchased during June	1,200 bottles
Total available during June	1,384 bottles
Deduct Stock remaining at 30 June	246 bottles
Number of bottles disposed of	1,138 bottles
Number of bottles sold	1,130 bottles
Discrepancy	8 bottles

This depends on knowing the number of bottles sold, which is difficult information to obtain, and will not cope with sales of mixed drinks like gin and tonic. Also there is no indication whether the discrepancy consists of eight splits of tonic water or eight magnums of champagne! To be useful as a control it must be possible to judge the seriousness of any discrepancy.

A similar calculation based on cost price of the goods will certainly be made in order to calculate the gross profit earned in the month. To some extent this will also control the stock, because any losses of stock will be reflected in a drop in gross profit percentage, but stock losses are not the only possible causes of a drop in gross profit percentage, and a separate control is needed. In order to compare like with like, this means expressing all values at selling price:

Opening stock at selling price	£115
Purchases	1,463
	1,578
Deduct Closing stock	82
Goods sold	1,496
Sales	1,507
Surplus (0·7%)	11

In making this calculation, allowance should be made for any known breakages or other losses, and if only one commodity were being sold it should be possible to reconcile exactly. This will not be possible in practice for various reasons, of which the sale of mixed drinks has the greatest effect. Bottles of beer and bottles of lemonade can individually be valued at selling price, but if sold as glasses of shandy may amount to a different selling price. Similarly a bottle of sherry may be valued at £3·25 because a glass of sherry is sold for £0·25 and a bottle will produce thirteen glasses. Nevertheless it sometimes happens that fourteen glasses will be produced out of a bottle and a discrepancy will thus occur. A bottle of gin can be calculated to produce thirty-two measures of gin, each selling for the same price, but the prices charged for gin and orange, gin and bitters, or neat gin will not be exactly in proportion to their ingredients. The effect of these inevitable discrepancies is normally to produce a surplus, that is the actual sales should be above the calculated figure. A different sales mix will produce a different result, but the discrepancy should be consistent. If there is no surplus, or the surplus is less than usual, investigation should be made into the cause, which may be loss of stock or loss of takings.

STOCKS AT SELLING PRICE

First consider the means of producing all the figures at selling price. With regard to purchases, an additional day book should be kept at selling price, while for stock-in-hand it will merely mean an extra column on the stock sheet, which will now show all quantities valued at both cost and selling price. The cost total will be needed for the periodical calculation of gross profit, and the selling price total for control purposes. The wine list will provide the selling price of each item, and opened bottles will be valued at the proportion remaining compared with the total number of glasses which can be produced from the bottle. Measuring sticks are available for this purpose which will readily estimate the number of glasses remaining in a bottle. It should be emphasized that the selling price of a bottle is the price it will be sold for. If it will be sold piecemeal at so much per glass, the selling price of the bottle will be the price per glass multiplied by the number of glasses contained in the bottle. Wines which are to be sold by the bottle are a different proposition and can be valued straight from the wine list.

ALLOWANCES

Where stock is being strictly controlled, it is necessary to make allowance in the control figures for any goods accounted for other than by sales.

Returns to suppliers do not fall into this category since they will have been dealt with automatically by deduction from purchases, but further adjustment may be necessary as a result of:

1. Breakages.
2. Transfers to kitchen or other departments.
3. Issues to staff.
4. Drawings by proprietors.

In all these cases it is a matter of adjusting for known discrepancies, so that any remaining discrepancy will be highlighted as needing investigation. Each item should be properly recorded on a transfer note (*see* Chapter 7) and for this purpose it is convenient to use the same form for breakages, although there will be no receiving department in that case.

EXERCISES

1. Briefly explain why the gross profit percentage expected from the sale of wines and spirits is different from that expected from the sale of meals.
2. Why is it important from a costing point of view to keep records of the purchase and sale of bar stocks separate from the purchase and sale of food?
3. Explain the method of controlling bar stocks at selling price. Why should a surplus be expected?
4. The following figures relate to the bar stocks of a restaurant for the month of June:

	Cost £	Selling price £
Sales		921
Purchases	440	880
Stock at 1 June	114	228
Stock at 30 June	99	198

Calculate:

(a) The gross profit percentage of sales.

(b) The calculated sales on control at selling price.

(c) The surplus as a percentage of calculated sales.

5. Prepare a bar control at selling price from the following information, showing the surplus percentage of goods sold at selling price:

	£
Opening stock at selling price	356
Closing stock at selling price	284
Purchases at selling price	1,001
Transfers in at selling price	84
Transfers out at selling price	37
Allowances	6
Sales	1,214

6. Outline a method of controlling a liquor bar and of establishing the value of the surplus or deficit at selling price over a period of time.

(H.C.I.M.A.)

7. For the purposes of control at selling price, you are required to value the following bar stock sheet at selling price. Spirits are to be taken as thirty-two measures per bottle, sherry at thirteen glasses per bottle, and carafe wine at six glasses per carafe.

Quantity	Details	Selling price	Value
3½ bottles	Whisky	30p per measure	
4 bottles	Gin	30p per measure	
4 bottles	Sherry	25p per glass	
12 carafes	Wine	35p per glass	
36 bottles	Table wine	£1·72 per bottle	

10. *Labour Cost*

LABOUR COST comprises all costs of employing staff, whether paid in cash or in any other way. From the weekly payroll will be included the total of gross pay, plus employer's contributions to National Insurance. In addition there may be casual labour payments made through petty cash, and monthly salaries including employer's contributions as for wages. These all add up to the total paid in cash for the employment of staff, but there will also be costs incurred in kind, for supplying meals and perhaps accommodation to staff. Staff meals are just as much a part of the remuneration to the staff as the cash wages paid to them, and higher cash wages would be demanded if meals were not supplied. From the employer's point of view a cost is being incurred for both cash payments and food payments, and both are incurred as a result of employing staff. Similarly, accommodation supplied to hotel staff living in is a cost incurred solely for the employment of staff, and must be included in any calculation of labour cost.

The result of ignoring any part of total labour cost is that consideration will only be given to part of the relevant facts, with the consequent likelihood of drawing wrong conclusions. For comparison purposes the make-up of the figures must be consistent, whether they are being compared with other periods of time, with other costs (such as considering the installation of machinery) or being expressed as a percentage of sales in order to evaluate the rate of gross profit. If an employee is paid £30 per week for one month, and then paid £22 per week plus £8 food and accommodation per week in the next month, the cost to the employer has remained the same, and his costing figures should show this. If they show any change, as they will if staff meals and accommodation are ignored, they will be misleading and possibly cause expensive mistakes.

We have already seen that the labour cost of a small unit of sales such as one dish will be allowed for by reference to the appropriate percentage of selling price. To establish *what is* the appropriate percentage, and to check that it remains appropriate, it is necessary to calculate the labour cost for certain periods of time. This will be done as a matter of course every month when preparing the regular figures of cost and profit, but since wages are paid every week, it is useful to have a weekly check on the labour cost by preparing a *weekly labour cost statement*.

WEEKLY LABOUR COST STATEMENT

A weekly labour cost statement should contain enough information to establish whether the labour cost for each revenue-earning department is reasonable, and if not, where the trouble lies. This means relating the cost to turnover by percentages, and also comparison with some past performance or budget. The question of budgets is dealt with in Chapter 15, but the important point here is to know whether the calculated labour cost percentage is reasonable. If the percentage achieved in the same week last year is to be taken as a yardstick by which to measure this week's result, then last year's percentages will be shown on the statement (*see* Figure 8).

In preparing the figures for this statement the question will arise of what should be done about holiday pay and sick pay. In both cases these are amounts paid to employees for periods in which they are not working, and if the payments are included in the cost for the week comparison with other weeks will be invalidated, yet the cost has to be met and must therefore be allowed for.

In attempting to answer this question it should be remembered that the object of a weekly labour cost statement is to detect quickly any serious overspending on what is the largest single item of cost after food cost. This is done by comparing the percentage of sales with a previously determined yardstick, and this will almost certainly not be the same percentage as is shown by the figures for the year. Any sort of seasonal influence will result in the labour cost for different weeks being different percentages, because labour cost is variable but not in direct proportion to sales. The wages percentage for the year of a seasonal business may be 28%, but the percentages during the year may very well be:

May	40%
June	35%
July	27%
August	22%

The low percentage on high sales in the season compensates for the high percentage out of season and produces 28% overall. From this it is reasonable to deduce that if the figures next year are comparable month by month or week by week, a comparable result overall will be achieved.

Moon Restaurant

Weekly labour cost statement

W/E *10ᵗʰ April 19..*

	£	%	Last year %
Sales	575	100·0	100·0
Kitchen	75	13·0	13·1
Dining room	57	9·9	10·6
Wash–up	24	4·2	4·1
Cleaners	11	1·9	1·8
	167	29·0	29·6

Notes :

Dining Room cost noted as "too high" on last year's Statement.

Figure 8. Weekly labour cost statement

It is the comparison that is more important than the actual amounts, and for this reason holiday pay and sick pay should be omitted from all weekly comparison figures. All figures will then be comparable and valid comparisons can be made.

INDIRECT LABOUR COST

When considering the costs of a single-unit business, such as a single restaurant, it is sufficient to deal with total labour cost in any calculation of costs and profit, since it must all be paid for out of the one source of income. Details will be required of how much relates to kitchen and how much to restaurant only in order to control the costs, not in order to calculate profit.

In a multiple-unit business, however, such as a multiple restaurant, restaurant with outside catering or banquets, restaurant and bar, or hotel with restaurant, bar, and accommodation, it becomes necessary to identify costs directly to the source of income to which they relate. To determine the profit made by each source the labour cost incurred to produce that profit must be determined, and a difficulty is immediately encountered in that some labour cost is direct and some is indirect. Some wages, such as for chefs, waiters, barmen, housekeepers or chambermaids, can readily be allocated to income from meals, wines, or accommodation; but managers, office staff, and maintenance men, for example, work for all departments, and the cost of their employment should be charged to all. It is indirect labour cost, which requires the same treatment as overheads in an hotel business. This is dealt with in Chapter 13.

BANQUET LABOUR COST

When preparing a special function it may be that staff are specially engaged for the occasion, in which case the direct labour cost can be ascertained without difficulty, or it may be that existing staff are utilized, with or without temporary assistance. In this case calculation of direct labour cost will involve apportionment of the wages of existing staff between normal duties and the special function. In both cases the cost will be higher than normal rates, since it will involve special rates for temporary staff or overtime rates for permanent staff. The costing figures should not be taken at just the normal percentage in respect of labour cost, but direct labour cost should be calculated exactly, and a percentage added to cover indirect labour cost.

EXERCISES

1. Briefly explain what is meant by labour cost and how it differs from wages.

2. Name three different items which may be included in the labour cost of a restaurant, and say from what source you would get information on the cost of each item.

3. A restaurant employs a manager at a salary of £3,900 per year, six kitchen staff for whom gross wages and employer's contributions amount to £180 per week, and four restaurant staff totalling £114 per week. All staff have meals supplied by the restaurant for six days per week, fifty weeks in the year. The cost of staff meals is 50p per person per day. In the four-week period ended on 28 June casual wages payments amounting to £36·00 were made through petty cash.

    Calculate the labour cost of the restaurant for the four weeks ended 28 June.

4. The sales of a restaurant for the week ended 17 May amount to £684. Wages for the week amounted to £134, proportion of salaries £26, and staff meals £18. Calculate the labour cost as a percentage of sales.

5. *(a)* Briefly explain the purpose of a weekly labour cost statement and describe how the use of comparative figures helps to achieve this purpose.

   (b) What is meant by 'the inclusive cost of labour'?

6. Explain the difference between direct labour cost and indirect labour cost. In what circumstances is the distinction important?

11. *Overheads*

OVERHEADS may be defined as those expenses which are not capable of being identified with a particular unit of sales, but which nevertheless form part of the total cost. In catering costs it is usual to treat as overheads all expenses other than food cost and labour cost.

In this connection the meaning of the word *expenses* should be clearly understood and distinguished from *expenditure*, which may include capital items. Expenses are those payments which are incurred in the course of running a business for which no asset is acquired. When expenditure is incurred in acquiring an asset there is no change in total wealth, there is merely a change in the kinds of asset comprising the total wealth. If a refrigerator is purchased for £100, part of the wealth represented by £100 in cash has been exchanged for £100 worth of refrigerator, leaving total wealth unchanged. When expenditure is incurred on expenses, on the other hand, there is a reduction in total wealth. It is hoped that the expenses incurred will result in receiving income of greater amount, in which case a profit will have been made and total wealth ultimately increased, but the expenses themselves reduce wealth. If they are allowed to become greater in amount than the income then a loss has been made. Expenses are not necessarily cash expenses, but may be reductions in the value of assets such as bad debts or depreciation of equipment.

Overhead expenses fall into two main groups, *fixed expenses* and *variable expenses*. In the first category will be included such items as rent, rates, insurance, depreciation, and mortgage interest, which are fixed in amount irrespective of how much business is done. In each case the amount of the expenses for the year is known, and apportionment of this amount to different parts of the year will depend only on how much time is involved, not on whether it is in season or out of season.

Variable expenses, as the term implies, will vary with the amount of turnover, although not necessarily in proportion. They may include such items as cleaning, laundry, breakages, and maintenance, but the classification may differ in different businesses according to circumstances. Thus the cost of light and heat may be such a constant amount as to be a fixed expense, or it may vary with the business done. Many items will in fact be semi-variable, in that a certain minimum cost is inevitable and beyond that point the amount will rise as more business is done. The importance of distinguishing between fixed and variable expenses lies in the assistance it gives in allocating costs to a unit of time, and particularly in budgeting for the future.

Some overhead expenses are common to all businesses, while others will be incurred by some businesses and not by others, but those most commonly incurred are as follows:

Rent
Rates
Insurance
Lighting and heating (gas, electricity, fuel)
Telephone
Postage, printing, and stationery
Advertising and display
Repairs and maintenance
Renewals
Cleaning and laundry
Motor expenses
Depreciation
Bank interest and charges
Loan interest
Interest on capital invested
Legal fees
Audit fees
Sundry expenses

APPORTIONMENT OF FIXED EXPENSES

We have already seen that the food cost will not be the amount purchased in the month, and labour cost will not be just the total from the payroll. Adjustments have to be made in order to find the amount of the cost relating to the month, and this is true also of overheads. Those overheads which are paid for a longer period than a month will need to be apportioned, so that the cost taken into account in the profit statement is the true cost for one month. Insurance will be paid for one year in advance, but each month of the year should bear its proportionate part of the cost, and only its proportionate part. This will mean taking into account one-twelfth of the insurance premium in each of eleven months when no insurance is actually paid, and deducting eleven-twelfths of the premium from the costs of the month in which it is paid. Similarly other fixed expenses should be apportioned, so that the profit statement for each month reflects the appropriate proportion of each. The method is to ascertain the total annual cost of each fixed expense and divide by twelve if the statement is for the period of a calendar month. If it is to be a four-week or five-week period, the annual cost should be divided by fifty-two to find the cost per week, and this amount multiplied by four or five.

Example

Rates amount to £1,248 p.a. and insurance to £160 p.a. What amounts for these expenses should be taken into operating statements for July (4 weeks), August (4 weeks), and September (5 weeks)?

Answer
The cost of rates amounts to exactly £24 per week, or £96 for a four-week period and £120 for a five-week period. The cost of insurance does not divide exactly, being £3$\frac{4}{52}$ per week, or £12$\frac{16}{52}$ for a four-week period and £15$\frac{20}{52}$ for a five-week period. These amounts will be rounded off, but the total of the three periods must amount to £40, or one-quarter of £160:

	July £	*August* £	*September* £
Rates	96	96	120
Insurance	12	12	16

TREATMENT OF OTHER EXPENSES

The heading *lighting and heating* covers the cost of gas, electricity, and fuel. If the amounts are large enough to be significant it will be necessary to deal with these separately. Gas and electricity bills are normally paid quarterly, but the cost for each month can be estimated if the meter readings are noted at the end of each period. Cost of fuel oil or solid fuel used during the month can be calculated in the same way as food cost, i.e. the cost of opening stock plus purchases, less closing stock.

Telephone accounts are paid quarterly, and include a charge for rental in advance and a charge for calls in arrear, but the rental is a constant amount and does not therefore cause an added difficulty.

Postage, printing, and stationery may include small amounts recurring throughout the year, and large amounts occurring perhaps only once in the year. In that case the charge for one month should be a proportion of the large amount added to the normal recurring items for a month.

Advertising and display may also include large items which relate to a whole season rather than to the particular month in which they are paid, and these amounts will require apportionment. Care must be taken, however, to include as costs of a period only revenue expenditure. Advertising signs or display fittings which will continue in use into later years are capital items and should not be included except by way of depreciation, unless the amounts are too small to be material.

Repairs and maintenance, renewals, and *motor expenses* are other expenses which may include a mixture of regular amounts and infrequent amounts. Re-painting the premises will probably be planned to take place before the season starts, but is an expense attributable to the whole season. Maintenance of equipment may be arranged under maintenance contracts which provide for a fixed sum payable each year to cover all maintenance of certain items of equipment. In such cases the maintenance contract usually leaves the cost of materials still to be paid for. The argument is that the most expensive item in maintenance is the labour involved, and a contract which provides for a fixed annual payment, however much maintenance becomes necessary, eliminates the uncertainty and risk of unexpected heavy costs. This is true, but from the point of view of relating costs to a particular period of time it again means adding a proportion of a fixed expense to the total of the variable expense. For this purpose it is helpful if in all these cases the fixed annual charges are recorded separately from the casual payments, and a due proportion transferred periodically in order to find the true cost to date.

Depreciation is the reduction in the value of an asset due to the passing of time, and is an expense which must not be overlooked just because it does not cause cash payments. In this connection a cash payment was made when the asset was bought, and it is merely a question of spreading the cost less residual value over all the years of the asset's 'life' instead of setting the whole cost against the profit of the first year. Whatever the method adopted for determining the amount of depreciation for the year, the apportionment to different periods during the year should be made on a time basis.

It is easy to appreciate that interest payable is an expense, whether it is paid to a bank for overdraft facilities, or to a building society or other lender in respect of a loan. However, *interest on capital invested* is also a cost which should be covered by sales, even though it is not so obvious, and is not actually paid out in cash. It represents the return which the proprietor should expect on the capital he himself has invested in the business, and which he would receive if he invested his money instead in shares or other securities. If he could expect to receive an average yield of 10% on other investments, but invests his money in a business, then it costs him 10% on the amount of his capital to do so, and this amount must be recovered before the business can be said to make a profit. There is no difference in the profit-earning of a business whether its financing is provided by the proprietor himself or from outside, and cost figures should show this. In both cases any calculation of profit should allow for the cost of financing.

Legal fees and *audit fees* are normally both fixed expenses to be apportioned on a time basis, but it should be noted that legal fees incurred in connection with the acquisition of new assets, such as new premises, are not expenses but additional costs of the asset.

Sundry expenses is a general heading to include those items which will not fit any of the other headings, and are not large enough or otherwise significant enough to warrant a separate heading. For this reason the cost of sundry expenses will not be significant, and will be accounted for as it arises, without apportionment, as a variable expense.

STATEMENT OF COSTS AND PROFIT

Once the various detailed cost figures for a month have been obtained, it will be necessary to include them in a *statement of costs and profit*. This will differ in appearance from the usual annual profit and loss account, but is exactly the same in principle. The food cost will first be deducted from takings in order to find the gross profit, then wages and overheads will be deducted to show the net profit. This is commonly set out in vertical form, with each main heading also expressed as a percentage of sales:

	£	%
Sales	2,800	100·0
Food cost	1,120	40·0
Gross profit	1,680	60·0
Labour cost	760	27·1
Overheads	610	21·8
	1,370	48·9
Net profit	£310	11·1%

The general layout, with six main headings starting with sales and ending with net profit, should be followed every time, inserting additional details where appropriate.

Example

From the following information prepare a statement of costs and profit for the month of June, showing what the amount of each main heading represents as a percentage of sales: sales £3,150; purchases of food £1,420; purchases returns £30; stock at 1 June £120; stock at 30 June £130; wages £695; National Insurance £70; rent and rates £130; insurance £15; depreciation £95; lighting and heating £86; van expenses £20; repairs and maintenance £64; renewals £40; laundry and cleaning £48; printing and stationery £30; telephone £20; advertising £15; professional fees £5; interest on capital £40; sundry expenses £12. The cost of staff meals is valued at £150.

Answer

STATEMENT OF COSTS AND PROFIT FOR JUNE

	£	%
Sales	3,150	100·0
Food cost		
Opening stock	120	
Purchases 1,420		
Less Returns 30	1,390	
	1,510	
Less Closing stock	130	
	1,380	
Less Staff meals	150	
	1,230	39·1
Gross profit	1.920	60·9
Labour cost		
Wages	695	
National Insurance	70	
Staff meals	150	
	915	29·0
Overheads		
Rent and rates	130	
Insurance	15	
Depreciation	95	
Lighting and heating	86	
Van expenses	20	
Repairs and maintenance	64	
Renewals	40	
Laundry and cleaning	48	
Printing and stationery	30	
Telephone	20	
Advertising	15	
Professional fees	5	
Interest on capital	40	
Sundry expenses	12	
	620	19·7
	1,535	48·7
NET PROFIT	£ 385	12·2

EXERCISES

1. The following figures were extracted from the books of the Apex Restaurant for the month of June: stock of food at 1 June £100; stock of food at 30 June £80; sales £2,100; purchases £800; wages and salaries £500; overheads £450. The value of staff meals was estimated at £60 for the month. Prepare a statement of cost and profit and calculate the net profit percentage of sales.

2. The following figures were extracted from the books of the Excel Restaurant for the month of March:

	£
Stock at 1 March	280
Purchases of provisions	890
Stock at 31 March	210
Wages	420
Rent	65
Gas and electricity	55
Depreciation	90
Repairs and renewals	55
Sundry expenses	25
Printing and stationery	15
Postage and telephone	25
Sales	1,900
Staff meals are valued at	60

Find:

(a) The gross profit.
(b) The net profit.
(c) The net profit as a percentage of sales.

3. The Haven Restaurant's figures for the month of April were as follows:

	£
Stock of food at 1 April	102
Purchases of food	797
Stock of food at 30 April	94
Wages	510
Rates	122
Gas and electricity	48
Repairs and renewals	60
Printing and stationery	15

Postage and telephone	25
Insurances	10
Sundry expenses	105
Sales	2,000
Staff meals are valued at	50

Prepare a profit statement showing the calculation of gross profit and net profit, and express these amounts as a percentage of sales.

4. The following figures were extracted from the books of a restaurant for the month of May:

	£
Sales	2,850
Purchases	1,085
Stock of food at 1 May	108
Stock of food at 31 May	70
Wages	521
Salaries	185
Rates	65
Insurance	14
Lighting and heating	45
Maintenance and repairs	80
Renewals	60
Depreciation	70
Office expenses	345
Staff meals are valued at	40

(a) Prepare a statement of costs and profit showing the amounts of the usual main headings of cost and profit.

(b) Express each of the amounts of the main headings as a percentage of sales.

5. The following figures have been extracted from the books of the Popular Restaurant for the month of January: Stock at 1 January £310; purchases of provisions £880; closing stock £265; wages £505; rent £160; gas and electricity £85; depreciation £80; repairs and renewals £45; postage and telephone £25; printing and stationery £10; sundry expenses £35; sales £2,200. Adjustment is to be made for staff meals £45.

Calculate the following as amounts and as percentages of sales:

(a) Gross profit.

(b) The main headings of cost.

(c) Net profit.

6. The following information has been extracted from the books of the Ibex Restaurant for the month of June. You are required to prepare a statement of costs and profit in tabular form showing the main headings of cost, and to calculate the following, together with the percentage they represent to sales:
(a) Gross profit.
(b) The main headings of cost.
(c) Net profit.
Also show the net profit per representative customer.

	£
Stock at 1 June	620
Purchases of provisions	1,790
Stock at 30 June	580
Staff meals	70
Wages	1,030
Rent	320
Gas and electricity	170
Depreciation	160
Repairs and renewals	90
Postage and telephones	50
Printing and stationery	20
Sundry expenses	70
Sales	4,400

The number of customers served during the month was 2,640.

7. The following information was extracted from the records of a waitress-service restaurant in respect of April 19..:

	£
Sales	1,800
Stock of provisions on 1 April	250
Stock of provisions on 30 April	238
Cash purchases	455
Credit purchases	263
Purchases returns	18
Salaries and National Insurance	92
Wages and National Insurance	291
Rent and rates	96
Gas and electricity	70
Repairs and depreciation	95
Miscellaneous expenses	67

Note: £70 of the cost of provisions consumed is to be regarded as the cost of staff meals.

You are required to express each of the following as a percentage of sales:

(a) Food cost.
(b) Labour cost.
(c) Overhead cost.
(d) Total cost.
(e) Net profit.

(H.C.I.M.A.)

12. *Hotel Takings*

INCLUSIVE CHARGES

CHARGES to guests in hotels are generally composite amounts, covering both the sale of meals and the provision of accommodation. It may be that only breakfast is included in the quoted tariff, other meals being quoted separately, or it may be that the quoted tariff is for *en pension* terms. In this case, if the restaurant is not open to non-residents, the charges for meals as separate amounts may never have been established. In all these cases the takings from guests will be of two kinds, food sales and accommodation charges, and it is not always easy to decide how much the takings of each kind amount to, let alone what costs are attributable to each.

There may also be additional takings, such as bar sales, but these will be charged separately and can be dealt with separately. The important difference is that the amount of such sales is known, whereas in the case of inclusive charges to guests the amount of each part of the charge may not be known.

Unless some attempt is made to split the inclusive charges to guests, it is useless to attempt any calculation of gross profit, which must be based on sales and cost of the item sold. Since a charge for accommodation and food cost have no bearing on one another, it follows that the result of deducting food cost from total takings has no meaning, and is certainly not gross profit. Such a result expressed as a percentage of total takings will be affected by the proportion of meals sales to accommodation charges, or sales mix.

In the past there has been a commonly used rule-of-thumb method of dividing total takings in the proportions two-thirds and one-third in an attempt to solve this problem of unknown sales mix. This is rather like trying to solve a problem by pretending it doesn't exist. The result of calculating gross profit using a sales figure equal to two-thirds of total takings is no more accurate than making the same calculation using total takings. The answer is smaller, but will be true only if the true sales mix is in the ratio 2:1, and if we knew this, no rule of thumb would be necessary.

CHARGES FOR MEALS

The answer must lie in finding some way of identifying the amount of food sales, and to do this, it will be necessary to make an evaluation of the selling price of meals supplied to guests. This may be done over a sample period in order to establish a fair average. A deduction from total takings on this basis will then provide a food sales figure, on which cost calculations can be based.

Evaluation of meals supplied can in some cases be made on the basis of the charge made for chance meals. Where the menu offered to hotel visitors is the same as a *table d'hôte* meal offered at £3·00, then it can fairly be said that £3·00 of the inclusive terms relates to that meal. This reasoning may suffice for all meals, but probably there will be no recognized charge for breakfast, and in hotels with no chance trade there will be no previously established charges at all.

In the case where a selling price has to be established for only one meal, this can be calculated from the food cost as described in Chapter 3, using the same gross profit percentage as for the other meals already priced. Otherwise the calculation of the selling price of meals will be a similar problem to that of a restaurant, and dealt with in a similar way. The main difference is that in an hotel the rate of gross profit necessary to cover restaurant costs and net profit is not so easy to establish.

It is first necessary to establish the average food cost of meals supplied to guests and for this purpose dish costings should be prepared for the normal cycle of menus. When the average food cost of each meal (breakfast, lunch, dinner) has been determined, before we can calculate the appropriate charge it will be necessary to determine what rate of gross profit is required, and this in turn depends on the costs and net profit to be covered by food takings as distinct from accommodation charges.

The allocation of hotel costs is dealt with in Chapter 13, and by considering the analysis of income and costs together a calculated answer can be arrived at, but it should be remembered that while costing figures can give useful guidance, they must not be allowed to over-rule reason and commonsense. It is possible to become over-reliant on calculation, when a little trial and error would be more effective. In this sense, we know that a gross profit of about 60% is likely to be reasonable, and experience will tell us approximately what prices are reasonable for the meals being served. By applying these two reasonable factors to the known food cost a balance between them can be determined.

Example

The average food cost for breakfast is 41p, for lunch 77p, and for dinner £1·27. Selling prices are not known, but it is thought that lunch of the kind served would be charged at about £1·75 in a restaurant, and dinner £3·25. A charge for breakfast can only be guessed, but if the ratios for lunch and dinner can be determined, breakfast can be calculated on the same basis.

Lunch – if food cost is 77p and charge is £1·75, then gross profit is 56%

Dinner – if food cost is £1·27 and charge is £3·25, then gross profit is 61%.

There is a discrepancy here, but on consideration it may be thought that a higher charge of £1·90 for lunch and a lower charge of £3·10 for dinner would not be unreasonable, and these would both give a gross profit of approximately 59%. Using this percentage on the food cost for breakfast would give a charge of £1·00, which again does not appear unreasonable.

Now a starting point has been found which can be used as a basis to work on. Certain assumptions have had to be made, but they have been seen to be reasonable assumptions, and the resultant scale of meal charges will be more realistic and accurately related to costs than an arbitrary decision. Also a rate of gross profit has been established for checking with actual results over a period of time.

It is a common argument that meals to residents should be priced lower than meals to non-residents, on the grounds that with residents the meal is not the only source of income to the hotel. This argument defeats itself. The total charges must still cover costs and profit, and if the income from one source is reduced, the income from another source must be increased. Why then should accommodation charges be artificially made higher than they need be, in order to make meal charges appear lower than they should be? Both should be self-supporting.

Example

Inclusive terms for an hotel guest are £77·00 per week. Selling price of meals is calculated to be £1·25 for breakfast, £2·25 for lunch, and £3·75 for dinner. How should the inclusive terms be apportioned between apartments and food?

Answer

Total charge to guest		£77·00
Charges for meals:		
Breakfast 7 × £1·25	£8·75	
Lunch 7 × £2·25	£15·75	
Dinner 7 × £3·75	£26·25	
		£50·75
Charge for accommodation		£26·25

In this example the inclusive charge £77·00 may be split between food takings £50·75 and apartments takings £26·25, and it will be noticed that the amounts are approximately in the proportions 2 : 1 mentioned earlier. However, it should be remembered that different guests at the hotel will be charged different amounts because of occupying different rooms. The food consumed will be the same, and the amount charged for food will be the same, but the charge for accommodation will be different.

Example

A guest occupying a different room is charged £66·50 per week. He will be paying £50·75 for food, as before, but only £15·75 for accommodation, the proportions in this case being approximately 3 : 1.

The above examples have both assumed guests taking full board, but the same hotel may very well be catering for guests who require only accommodation and breakfast, or accommodation, breakfast, and dinner. In these cases the proportions of the total charge will be very different, and when the total takings for a week are considered, the amount will be a mixture of charges with different proportions, and the mixture will be different each week.

To split the total with some accuracy is a problem with two workable solutions. In both cases it is necessary to calculate the charge for food for each kind of booking, the first method being to make the allocation when first entering each inclusive charge, and the second method being to make the allocation in total at the end of a period.

Method 1

When recording the charge in the tabular ledger (or in a small hotel with no tab., in the cash received book), the total should be split between accommodation and food straight away. The appropriate amount for food is first entered in the food column, and the balance entered in the accommodation column. This is the more accurate method and means that takings are identified from the beginning.

TABULAR LEDGER

Room No.	Name	Terms	No. of guests	Accom	Food	Lunch
		£		£	£	£
10	White	9·50	2	6·00	13·00	
3	Smith	9·50	2	6·00	13·00	
18	Brown	9·25	1	2·75	6·50	
12	Jones	4·00	2	6·00	2·00	

Figure 9. Tabular ledger entries

In the example shown in Figure 9, full meals are assumed to be priced at £6·50 per person per day, of which breakfast is £1·00. Room 18, occupied by Mr Brown, is charged at a lower rate than the others because the room is not so attractive. Consequently the income for apartments is reduced, not the income for food. In Room 12, Mr and Mrs Jones are booked for bed and breakfast, and accordingly the room charge is the same as rooms 10 and 3, but the food charge is less. Where weekly terms are less than the equivalent daily terms the same principle should still be followed, the reduction being taken on apartments. With a weekly booking the costs which are less, such as laundry, are costs of providing accommodation, for which the charge can reasonably be reduced.

Method 2

At the end of each week or month the total food sales should be calculated by multiplying the meal charges per day by the number of
sleeper nights. This term is used to make allowance for the fact that
different visitors will have different lengths of stay, so that any calculation 'per visitor' must be adjusted to 'per visitor per night', which
is shortened to 'per sleeper night'. In this sense one visitor who stays
for 6 nights will constitute 6 sleeper nights. Two visitors who stay 3
days will also constitute 6 sleeper nights. Two visitors who stay for a
full week will constitute 14 sleeper nights.

Example

In one week: 7 visitors stayed 1 night each for bed and breakfast.
             3 visitors stayed 2 nights each for bed and breakfast.
             40 visitors stayed 7 nights each for full board.
  If the price of breakfast is £1·00, and full meals £6·00, then the
takings for food in a week will be £1·00 multiplied by the number of
bed-and-breakfast sleeper nights, plus £6·00 multiplied by the number
of full-board sleeper nights.

	£
Bed-and-breakfast sleeper nights:	
7 × 1 plus 3 × 2, total 13 @ £1·00 =	£13·00
Full-board sleeper nights:	
40 × 7, total 280 @ £6·00 =	£1,680·00
Total food sales for the week	£1,693·00

OCCUPANCY

When considering the income of an hotel, one important factor is the
rate of occupancy, expressed as a percentage of full occupancy, which
is the maximum number of sleeper nights possible for the hotel to
accommodate in a given period. Thus an hotel may have 50 bedrooms
capable of accommodating 90 guests each night. For one week full
occupancy would be 630 sleeper nights.
  If the same hotel has 40 of its rooms occupied by 70 guests for the
whole of one week, and 14 guests stay one night each in the other 10
rooms (some are double rooms), then the actual occupancy is 70 × 7
+ 14 = 504 sleeper nights. This expressed as a percentage of full

occupancy (630 sleeper nights) gives an occupancy rate of 80% for the week.

It should be remembered that it is possible to have every room occupied and not have 100% occupancy, if not every room is *fully* occupied. Hence the need for using sleeper nights, instead of the number of rooms, in the calculation.

EXERCISES

1. The Atlas Hotel charges £64·00 per week inclusive terms, and provides *table d'hôte* menus for non-residents at £2·20 for lunch and £2·80 for dinner. The selling price of breakfast is calculated at 80p.
   Calculate:
   (a) The split of the inclusive terms between meals and accommodation.
   (b) The nightly charge for bed and breakfast.

2. Dish costings of typical menus for the Bay Hotel show that the average cost of ingredients is as follows:

Breakfast	£0·348
Lunch	£1·278
Dinner	£1·734

   Accommodation charges for rooms at the hotel average £31·20 per week, and it is desired that the sale of meals shall produce a gross profit of 60%. What inclusive charge per person per week will produce the desired result?

3. The total takings of an hotel for a week amounted to £2,363·20. During the week 38 guests stayed 7 nights each for full board, 5 guests stayed 1 night each for bed and breakfast, and 8 guests stayed 2 nights each for bed and breakfast. Charges for meals are: breakfast 80p, lunch £2·20, and dinner £2·80.
   Calculate:
   (a) The total food takings for the week.
   (b) The average charge for accommodation per sleeper night.

4. The Haven Hotel has 40 bedrooms comprising 30 double rooms and 10 single rooms. During the week ending 30 June, 48 guests stayed for 7 nights each and 7 guests stayed 1 night each. Calculate the hotel's percentage occupancy for the week.

5. The charges for meals included in inclusive terms at the Key Hotel amount to £7·00 per day. During the week ended 10 July, 35 guests were charged £75·00 per week, 8 guests were charged £80·00 per week, and 3 guests were charged £85·00 per week. What was the average charge for accommodation per sleeper night?

13. *Hotel Costs*

HAVING apportioned the takings, it will be possible to compare food cost with food sales, but full costing means also checking labour costs and expenses, of which some will be directly attributable to the provision of meals, but others will be more general and relating to the hotel as a whole. This means that complete costing for meals will not be possible unless these other costs are apportioned.

We have so far made no attempt to cost the supply of accommodation, and this can also be attempted if general costs are apportioned, so that the profitability of this source of income can be determined.

This brings us to the basic need, which is the allocation of expenses to income. Whatever method of apportionment is adopted, it must have as its basis the relationship of the different sources of income out of which the expenses must be met. In a restaurant which sells only food, the income from selling food must be sufficient to pay all expenses and leave a profit. If the sale of drinks is added, then this must pay for its due proportion of expenses and profit. In an hotel there may very well be three main sources of income: accommodation, restaurant, and bar. Each will have its own direct expenses and each must provide enough income to cover its due proportion of general expenses and profit.

In allocating the expenses to the appropriate sources of income, the direct expenses are easily recognized and dealt with. Restaurant purchases and bar purchases can be kept separate and related to the correct source of income. Where goods are purchased for one source and used by another (e.g. potato crisps included in food purchases but sold in the bar) it is a comparatively simple matter to record such transfers daily and adjust the figures accordingly.

Wages of kitchen and restaurant staff can be earmarked to the restaurant. Bar staff, housekeepers, and chambermaids can all be directly related to appropriate sources of income and their wages charged accordingly. When the wages of all the staff who can be directly identified with particular sources of income have been dealt with, there will remain some wages for staff who are concerned with the business as a whole. These will include management, office staff, maintenance staff, porters, and front office staff, and the wages or salaries of all these will need apportioning in some way. Similarly some expenses can be directly identified to the restaurant, bar, or accommodation, whereas others relate in a general way to all three and need apportioning.

APPORTIONMENT BASED ON TAKINGS

The first method of apportionment which suggests itself is a division in proportion to sales. This has the merit of simplicity, and in many circumstances it will appear equitable that the greater part of the hotel expenses should be set off against the biggest turnover.

Example

The takings of an hotel amount to £110,000, divided as to rooms £38,000, meals £61,000, and bar £11,000. After allocating all expenses which could be directly related to each department, it is necessary to apportion wages amounting to £5,500 and overheads amounting to £8,800, the amounts being divided in proportion to sales.

Answer

The amount applicable to each department will be the total expense divided by total sales multiplied by the sales of the department:

Wages

$$\text{Rooms proportion} = \frac{\text{total wages} \times \text{rooms takings}}{\text{total takings}}$$

$$= \frac{£5,500 \times £38,000}{£110,000} = £1,900$$

$$\text{Meals proportion} = \frac{£5,500 \times £61,000}{£110,000} = £3,050$$

$$\text{Bar proportion} = \frac{£5,500 \times £11,000}{£110,000} = £\ 550$$

$$£5,500$$

$$\text{Overheads}$$

Rooms proportion $\quad=\quad \dfrac{£8,800 \times £38,000}{£110,000} \quad=\quad £3,040$

Meals proportion $\quad=\quad \dfrac{£8,800 \times £61,000}{£110,000} \quad=\quad £4,880$

Bar proportion $\quad=\quad \dfrac{£8,800 \times £11,000}{£110,000} \quad=\quad £\ \ 880$

$$£8,800$$

Ideally the correct method of apportionment is one which will be equitable in all circumstances, and unfortunately this will not always be true of using a takings ratio. The incidence of duty on drinks and tobacco, for instance, can substantially affect the selling price of these commodities, without any alteration of the trade itself or use of hotel facilities, and apportionment of expenses on a takings basis would mean that a higher proportion of overheads would now be attributed to the bar.

Since the gross profit on tobacco is only about 8% of takings, on wines about 50% of takings, on food about 60% of takings and on rooms 100% of takings, it is apparent that the gross profit out of which expenses must be met is nothing like in proportion to the takings of each department. If, however, the expenses are allocated in proportion to takings it would have the effect of unduly reducing bar net profit and inflating the net profit on accommodation.

Another objection is that as sales figures vary from period to period, the proportions will change for allocation of expenses. The expenses themselves, such as rates, may not change, but the amount of rates charged to one department will alter because the takings proportions have changed, even though the department continues to occupy the same amount of hotel. This leads to a better method of apportionment, described later, which is based on how much of the hotel is occupied by each department.

ALLOCATION BASED ON TIME SPENT

It may be possible to allocate indirect wages and salaries to different departments on the basis of time spent on work relating to those departments, as recorded in time-sheets or diaries.

To the extent that this is possible the effect is to convert these costs to direct labour cost and no further difficulty arises. Where any balance of labour cost is impossible to allocate in this way it may be arbitrarily apportioned, if of small amount, or dealt with by one of the other methods.

APPORTIONMENT BASED ON DIRECT LABOUR COST

This is an arbitrary allocation which would not have a wide application in hotels and restaurants, but may be suitable in certain circumstances.

METERING

Gas, electricity, and water charges are all based on metered supplies to the establishment, and the allocation of the cost may be achieved by installing subsidiary meters to each department. This again has the effect of turning an indirect expense into a direct expense to a very large extent, leaving only supplies to service areas to be allocated by some other method.

APPORTIONMENT ON BASIS OF FLOOR AREA

The expenses which need to be apportioned are those which relate to the hotel as a whole, rather than to any one department and it would therefore be appropriate to charge these expenses in proportion to the amount of hotel actually used by each department. In the case of rates, the hotel will pay more if it covers a large area, or less if it is smaller. The same principle can be applied in allocating not only rates but all other general overheads to the different departments within the hotel. If the floor area occupied by each source of income is estimated, the overheads can be apportioned on this basis, and the basis will not change for any reason but a change in the use of the hotel. Once the proportions have been agreed, they will remain unaltered except for building extensions or similar changes.

The floor areas to use will be those used exclusively for the purpose of each source of income. Any part of the hotel which is not exclusive to a particular source will be ignored, since the expenses relating to that part will need allocating to all the sources. This means that in an hotel with a restaurant and kitchen, bar, public rooms, reception, offices, and service areas on the ground floor, and bedrooms on the first and second floors, the allocation would be as follows:

Restaurant: floor area of restaurant, kitchen, still room.

Bar: floor area of bar and wine cellar.

Rooms: floor area of the whole of the first and second floors.

If the expenses were apportioned to the whole floor area including service areas, and the expenses of the service areas thus allocated were then apportioned between the three sources of income, the result is exactly the same as ignoring the floor area of service areas in the first place, as above. With regard to service areas on the first and second floors, these should be included with rooms since they serve no other purpose. The part of the whole hotel occupied by rooms includes the whole of the two upper floors, in which the restaurant and bar have no interest. On the other hand a lounge, for instance, serves restaurant, bar, and accommodation.

Example

An hotel has all its bedrooms on the first and second floors, a restaurant, bar, and public rooms on the ground floor.

Floor areas are as follows:

		sq. m
Ground floor	Restaurant	1,600
	Kitchens	1,200
	Bar and wine cellar	600
	Lounge	900
	Reception, offices, corridors, etc.	800
First floor	Bedrooms	4,400
	Corridors, service areas, etc.	700
Second floor	Bedrooms	4,000
	Corridors, service areas, etc.	500

Wages and expenses for the month of June have been allocated to restaurant, bar or rooms, as far as possible, but some costs relate to the hotel generally and should be apportioned on a floor-area basis. The amounts are as follows:

	£
Wages chargeable to:	
Restaurant	840
Bar	80
Rooms	120
General wages	260
	£1,300
Expenses chargeable to:	
Restaurant	130
Bar	20
Rooms	40
General overheads	910
	£1,100

Find the total wages and total overheads chargeable to each department of the hotel.

Answer

The relative floor areas are restaurant 2,800 sq. m, bar 600 sq. m, and rooms 9,600 sq. m, a total of 13,000 sq. m.

	Rest.	Bar	Rooms
Direct wages	840	80	120
General wages propn.			
$\dfrac{2,800}{13,000} \times £260$	56		
$\dfrac{600}{13,000} \times £260$		12	
$\dfrac{9,600}{13,000} \times £260$			192
Total wages	£896	£92	£312

Direct expenses	130	20	40

General overheads propn.

$$\frac{2,800}{13,000} \times £910 \qquad 196$$

$$\frac{600}{13,000} \times £910 \qquad\qquad\qquad 42$$

$$\frac{9,600}{13,000} \times £910 \qquad\qquad\qquad\qquad 672$$

Total expenses	£326	£62	£712

EXERCISES

1. Explain why it is necessary to determine the split of an hotel's costs between those relating to meals and those relating to accommodation.
2. Why should service areas be ignored when allocating expenses to sources of income on the basis of floor area?
3. General overheads of the Pioneer Hotel amount to £8,475 and it is required to allocate this amount to rooms, restaurant, and bar in proportion to their respective floor areas. These are as follows:

Bedrooms	4,100 sq. m
Restaurant and kitchen	1,050 sq. m
Bar	500 sq. m
Lounge	300 sq. m
Service areas	1,500 sq. m

Show the amount to be allocated to each source of income.

4. An hotel calculates that the costs attributable to bedrooms in a year amount to £8,176.

There are 40 bedrooms in the hotel accommodating a maximum of 70 guests, and the average occupancy rate is 64%. You are required to calculate the amount which must be charged per sleeper night to cover the cost of accommodation.

5. The Heather Hotel has a maximum occupancy of 420 sleeper nights per week, and average occupancy is 70%. Direct labour cost attributable to rooms amounts to £11,000 p.a., direct expenses

£6,000 p.a., and the appropriate proportion of general overheads is £29,000 p.a.

Calculate:

(a) The cost of accommodation per sleeper night.

(b) The charge per sleeper night necessary to produce a net profit on accommodation of 15% on sales.

6. The Ajax Hotel has 30 bedrooms, a bar, and a restaurant. Full occupancy is 385 sleeper nights per week, and average occupancy is 70%.

Floor areas are as follows:

Bedrooms	3,100 sq. m
Restaurant and kitchen	900 sq. m
Bar	400 sq. m
Lounge	200 sq. m
Service areas	1,000 sq. m

Direct wages for 5 full-time restaurant staff amount to £195 per week. Direct wages for 5 full-time house staff amount to £172 per week. Direct wages for 2 full-time bar staff amount to £54 per week. Direct expenses amount to £9,893 for house, £8,350 for restaurant, and £900 for bar.

Overheads amount to £26,400 p.a., including labour cost of management and service staff.

Net profit required on accommodation 15%.

Calculate what average charge per week must be made for accommodation.

7. The Golden Hotel has 40 bedrooms with a maximum occupancy of 490 sleeper nights per week. Average occupancy is 60% throughout the year.

Meals provided to guests have been costed, and the average food cost is as follows:

Breakfast	£0·36
Lunch	£1·10
Dinner	£1·34

Direct wages and staff meals are as follows:

Restaurant and kitchen	£343·00
Housekeeping	£195·20 per week
General	£176·00 per week

Direct expenses are £4,576 p.a. for housekeeping, and £5,200 p.a. for the restaurant. Indirect expenses amount to £34,112, which should be apportioned on the basis of floor area.

Floor areas of the hotel are:

Bedrooms	3,600 sq. m
Restaurant	1,200 sq. m
Service areas, etc.	600 sq. m

A net profit of 10% must be made on both restaurant takings and accommodation takings. You are required to calculate what inclusive terms should be charged per week, and the split between meals and accommodation.

14. Small Hotels

THE principles governing costing for small hotels are no different from those for large hotels, but certain difficulties do arise from not having the same book-keeping facilities. The annual accounts of a small hotel will probably be prepared by an outside accountant who has been asked to do no more than agree the profit with the Inspector of Taxes, and the figure of takings shown will consist of inclusive charges without any dissection between accommodation charges and sales of meals.

On the other hand, because there is not so much complexity as in the larger hotels, it may be possible in some cases to obtain sufficient information without splitting inclusive charges into their component parts. The factor that makes such a split necessary normally is sales-mix variation, which invalidates comparison of total amounts. But small hotels, which might find the effort to analyse takings and expenses irksome, are precisely the businesses which may have a constant sales mix. They may very well cater only for full-board guests staying on weekly terms, and if this is so then useful comparisons can be made on total figures. Proportions will be different from those applying elsewhere, but will be constant for the business concerned.

The profit and loss account of a typical small hotel is illustrated at Figure 10. It will be seen that takings are shown in one amount £33,000, and the only other item on the credit side of the account is 'own accommodation' £600. This is an estimate of the value of food and accommodation provided for the proprietor and his family by the business, and included in the expenses on the debit (left-hand) side of the account. In calculating the profit of the business it would be wrong to set off all the expenses against the takings, including the proportion of the expenses attributable to the proprietor's private accommodation.

On the debit side of the account the expenses are shown under the usual headings, but no attempt has been made to strike a figure of gross profit. Since the takings do not show food sales separately this cannot be done, and for the same reason it has not been thought

THE PERSPEX HOTEL

Profit and Loss Account for Year ended 30th Sept 19..

	£		£
Food Purchases	10,500	Takings	33,000
Wages	8,450		
Rates	1,250	Own Accommodation	600
Insurance	150		
Light and Heat	2,500		
Laundry and Cleaning	550		
Repairs and Renewals	1,250		
Advertising	200		
Telephone	180		
Printing and Stationery	170		
Bank Charges and Interest	800		
Sundry Expenses	350		
Depreciation	900		
	27,250		
Net profit	6,350		
	33,600		33,600

Figure 10. A profit and loss account for a small hotel

necessary to evaluate the staff meals. This form of account is perfectly adequate for such purposes as agreeing an assessment to Income Tax, where all that is required is the amount of net profit achieved, and some detail as to how it was arrived at, but for costing purposes it lacks those comparisons and ratios which are necessary in order to put the information to future use.

Let us first of all summarize the information given and insert the percentage of sales for each heading:

		£
Takings	100%	33,000
Food cost	32%	10,500
Wages	26%	8,450
Overheads	25%	8,300

		£
	83%	27,250
Less Own accommodation	2%	600
	81%	26,650
Net Profit	19%	6,350

FOOD COST AS A PERCENTAGE OF TOTAL TAKINGS

We have already said that since the takings include accommodation as well as meals, the cost of food has no direct relationship with total takings. To find a true gross profit we should have to split the takings into the component parts, and we should also have to deduct staff and proprietor's meals from the cost of food. In these circumstances, is any value to be obtained from discovering that the food cost amount is 32% of the total takings? The answer is yes, within certain well-defined limits, beyond which the information will be misleading:

(a) The percentage will be useful only for comparing the figures of one period with another period, not for comparison with other businesses.

(b) The sales mix must remain in constant proportions, e.g. terms must be, and remain, only full board or only bed and breakfast, not a mixture of the two.

(c) The effect of staff and proprietor's meals must not change materially or adjustment for this will have to be made.

In these circumstances the percentage food cost on total takings will be valid for comparison of one year with another, for estimating future results, and for dish costing of menus. There will be a need to compare the cost of food supplied to guests in a week with the charges for a week, instead of the food cost of one dish with the selling price of that dish, and the ratio used for comparison will not be the gross profit percentage, but food cost percentage of total takings.

Example

The annual accounts of a small hotel show that food cost for the year amounts to 35% of total takings. If the average weekly charge is £55·00, what amount can be spent on food each week in order to achieve the required result over the year?

Answer

$$35\% \text{ of } £55\cdot00 \text{ is } \frac{35}{100} \times \frac{£55\cdot00}{1} = £19\cdot25$$

This means that the food cost per guest for the week can be £19·25 in order to achieve the required result. The meals to be supplied during the week should each be dish-costed to find the food cost per cover, and the total for the week compared with £19·25.

It may be true that the food cost would be 44% of meals takings if these were known, whereas it is being shown as 35% of total takings, but while total takings are greater than meal takings by the *same proportion*, the food cost percentage should appear as 35% for any level of takings, provided that the food cost itself remains proportionate. This will then provide guidance whether food cost is remaining at a reasonable level, by comparing the percentages of consecutive periods.

REVISION OF INCLUSIVE CHARGES

To plan any scale of charges for the future, it is necessary to forecast what costs and profit must be covered by the charges, and divide the total by the number of sales units.

Example

A small hotel is open only during the season for a period of fifteen weeks. It is expected that average occupancy will be thirty-eight guests per week for the fifteen weeks.

Specimen menus have been costed, and food cost is expected to be £14·00 per week per guest.

Wages will be payable to four full-time staff at £35·00 each per week, and to two part-time staff at £15·00 each per week. The proprietor and his wife will be fully employed in the business during the season, and remuneration for their work should be allowed for at £100 per week.

Staff meals for all full-time staff and proprietors should be valued at £3·50 per person per week.

Overheads are expected to amount to £12,640, but in addition interest on capital (£20,000) must be allowed for at 10% p.a.

It is desired to produce a net profit of £4,000 in addition to a return for own labour and capital.

BUDGET FOR THE COMING YEAR

		£
Food cost (38 guests p.w. for 15 weeks @ £14)		7,980
Labour cost:		
Wages 4 × £35 × 15 wks.	2,100	
2 × £15 × 15 wks.	450	
Self £100 × 15 wks.	1,500	
Meals 6 × £3·50 × 15 wks.	315	
		4,365
Overheads		
Estimate	12,640	
Add Interest on capital 10% of £20,000	2,000	
		£14,640
Net Profit required		4,000
Total takings to be provided by 570 guests		£30,985
Charge per guest per week (£30,985 ÷ 570)		£54·36
say		£55·00

BOOK-KEEPING FOR SMALL HOTELS

The figures we have considered above appeared in the annual profit and loss account, and it now remains to discover how the proprietor of a small hotel can obtain monthly figures for comparison purposes. If he already keeps a full set of book-keeping books there will be no problem, but if not it will still be possible to obtain perfectly satisfactory information by keeping an analysed cash book. An example of this is illustrated in Figure 11, the principle being that in addition to a column on either side (marked 'total') to record money being received or paid, there are also other columns to provide information about the nature of the transaction. When a payment is made in respect of a food purchase, as in the illustration on 7 April – the payment of £142 to Stewards Ltd – it is entered in the 'total' column

		Takings	Sundries	Total			Total	Food purchases	Wages	Cleaning and laundry	Repairs and renewals	Light and heat	Rates Insurance t'phone	Adverts post stat'ny	Sundry Expenses	Misc
April 1	Balance B/Fwd		848	848	April 4	Premier Stationary	4							4		
8	Takings	392		392	6	Corporation Rates	406						406			
15	Takings	465		465	7	Stewards Ltd	142	142								
22	Takings	488		488		Creamier Dairies	67	67								
29	Takings	485		485		Cash and Carry	83	83								
						Post Office phone	96						95			
					8	Wages	115		115							
					12	F. Smith Ltd	52	52								
						White Laundries	46			46						
						Window Cleaners	13			13						
						Gas	81					81				
						Electricity	117					117				
					15	Wages	115		115							
					17	Petty Cash	19	3			16					
					20	Electricity Board (Hoover)	56									56
					22	Wages	115		115							
					25	Cash and Carry	79	79								
					29	Wages	115		115							
							1720	426	460	59	16	198	501	4		56
					30	Balance c/fwd.	958									
		1830	848	2678			2678									
May 1	Balance B/fwd.		958	958												

Figure 11. An analysed cash book

to record the payment and also in the 'food purchases' column to enable the purchases to be added easily. Similarly, all other payments are analysed, and at the end of the month all the analysis columns are added to show the total of each kind of expense paid in the month.

It should be remembered that these are amounts paid *in* the month, and are not necessarily expenses *of* the month. For the calculation of gross profit, or indeed for any costing purpose, it is necessary to relate expenses to the income with which they are connected, in this case the expenses incurred in April related to the takings earned in April. Food purchase payments will need adjusting to include amounts still unpaid at the end of the month, and to exclude amounts paid for last month's purchases. If goods are bought on monthly account, most of the payments will be in respect of last month's purchases.

With regard to takings, the amount earned in April will be the charges for guests staying in the hotel in April. Some of these charges will have been paid as deposits in earlier months, some will have been paid in April, and some will still be due at the end of the month for guests who are still staying at the hotel. The amount actually received in April will include some charges in respect of guests in March, and some deposits for bookings in later months. The adjustment necessary to arrive at the takings for April will be as follows:

Takings during April		£1,830
Add: Deposits for April bookings	28	
April charges not yet received	180	
	—	208
		2,038
Deduct: March charges received in April	243	
Deposits in advance	64	
	—	307
Takings for April		£1,731

EXERCISES

1. The annual accounts for a small hotel show takings £27,500; food purchases £8,250; wages and expenses £15,250; and net profit £4,000.

Find:

(a) The food cost percentage of takings.

(b) The amount which can be spent on food per person each week if the average weekly charge is £58·00.

2. Total takings of a small hotel during June amounted to £2,550, including deposits for bookings in later months amounting to £60 and May accounts £570 received in June. Deposits for June bookings previously received amounted to £180, and at 30 June visitors' accounts due amounted to £660. Calculate the takings for June.

3. The following information relates to a small hotel:

	£
Total takings during the month of July	2,000
July deposits received in January	180
August deposits included in July takings	70
June takings received in July	540
July takings received in August	630
Purchases of food paid for in July	690
Purchase accounts owing at 1 July	650
Purchase accounts owing at 31 July	710

Assuming that stocks of food were negligible, calculate:

(a) Takings for July.

(b) Food purchases for July.

(c) Food purchases as a percentage of takings.

4. Name three items of cost which must be recovered from takings but which are not paid for in cash. Explain how these costs arise.

5. The Haven Hotel makes average charges of £60·00 per week, and expects to have 600 visitors each staying one week next year. Cost of food is expected to be £12,800, labour cost £7,600, and overheads £9,200 including loan interest paid. In addition allowance should be made for interest at 10% on the proprietor's capital £20,000 employed in the business, and a return of £3,000 for proprietor's own labour.

Calculate:

(a) What net profit for engaging in business is being made in addition to return for own labour and capital invested.

(b) What charge per week would have to be made in order to achieve a net profit of £2,000 p.a.

15. *Profit Budgets*

THE term 'budget' is here used to mean a carefully estimated forecast of future financial transactions: the preparation of budgets enables future results to be foreseen and plans to be made accordingly. It also enables actual results to be compared with the budgets, so that variations can be investigated and prompt action taken if necessary. This comparison of actual figures with budget figures in order to instigate management action is known as *budgetary control.*

Budgets may be prepared for any function represented by accounting statements to management, but will be of two main kinds: *revenue budgets* and *capital budgets.* The former are concerned with items of income and expense, or profit-making, while capital budgets will be concerned with changes in assets and liabilities. Of capital budgets the most widely used are cash budgets and cash flow statements, which will be dealt with in the next chapters.

Revenue budgets may be prepared for individual items of income and expense, in as much detail as may be required, or may be prepared for all such items in one statement, thus producing an estimated figure of profit. It will be found useful if this profit budget is prepared for the coming year and for each month of the year, the total of the monthly estimates for each item being the annual estimate for that item. Some amounts will be easier to estimate first as an annual figure, afterwards allocating the total to the different months, while others will be easier to estimate one month at a time.

In this connection it soon becomes apparent that calendar months are unsatisfactory units of time when comparisons are to be made. Months comprising different numbers of days and ending on different days of the week cause complications in allocating costs and in interpreting results. The difficulty is usually overcome in one of two ways:

First Method

The year is divided into thirteen accounting periods of four weeks each, so that every accounting 'month' is always comparable in terms of time with every other month. This has many advantages for estimation or comparison, but involves working with accounting periods which end at odd times in a calendar month.

For example, if the accounting year commences on 1 January, the accounting periods would be as follows:

Accounting period	1	4 weeks ending 28 January
	2	25 February
	3	25 March
	4	22 April
	5	20 May
	6	17 June
	7	15 July
	8	12 August
	9	9 September
	10	7 October
	11	4 November
	12	2 December
	13	30 December

The next accounting year commences on 31 December, being the same day of the week but a different date.

Second Method

The year is divided into twelve accounting periods of four or five weeks, each quarter comprising one period of five weeks and two of four weeks. Each period ends on the same day of the week, which will be the nearest to the end of the calendar month. This method means that not all months within the year are comparable in length of time, but each month can be directly compared with the same month in the previous year.

The first essential of any budget is that it shall be a forecast of happenings in the future, which means that some reasonable basis of estimation must be found.

Where figures exist in respect of previous years, these will provide a starting point for estimation for the coming year. The estimate should take into account the effect of all known circumstances which would make the coming year's figures different, such as increases in turnover due to more extensive advertising, extensions to premises, or additional conferences to be held in the town. National pay awards, or increases in National Insurance will cause higher wages costs. Changes in electricity or gas charges, reduced maintenance costs due to purchases of new equipment, but increased depreciation in consequence, should all be taken into account. By this means the income and costs for next year can be estimated by reference to the increase or reduction expected on last year's figures, an alteration to a figure being easier to estimate than the figure itself. Note that determination is itself a circumstance which can make next year's figures different from last year's. Turning off a gas ring, or forgetting to, can have more effect on the gas bill than a change in gas charges.

Where no previous figures exist, as in a new business, estimation is more difficult and more subject to error. This should not be taken as a discouragement, but the liability to error should be recognized and acknowledged. The budget figure which differs from the actual figure eventually achieved draws attention to the circumstances and increases our knowledge of the factors involved. It may be that we have over- or underestimated, or it may be that the estimate was reasonable, and the actual got out of hand. Either way it is useful to find out.

As before, the estimates should take into account all known facts, but without any previous figures to use as a basis, the best starting point would be 'maximum possible sales'. A restaurant can estimate maximum sales from the number of available place settings and an average charge per customer. An hotel can calculate maximum sales from the number of beds available and the average charge per guest. In each case the maximum figures should be adjusted by the reduction expected. The actual occupancy of an hotel measured in bed nights compared with the maximum bed nights is usually expressed as a percentage and referred to as 'an $x\%$ occupancy'.

Once takings have been estimated, gross profit can be estimated as a percentage, using approximately 60% as a guide. Experience will show in due time a more accurate percentage for future use.

Wages should be estimated in terms of how many staff will be needed and their rate of pay, not forgetting to allow for employer's contributions to National Insurance, etc. The amount thus calculated should also be compared with estimated takings to see that the percentage is reasonable.

Fixed expenses can be forecast exactly, but variable expenses must be estimated as well as possible. Again, comparison with sales as a percentage will provide some guidance.

Net profit is the amount remaining after deducting the wages and overheads from gross profit. The amount should be examined to see that it is reasonable, and if not the other estimates should be looked at again to see what alteration would produce a reasonable net profit and whether this alteration could reasonably be achieved. The constant emphasis on being reasonable should not be overlooked. However wrong it is subsequently proved, a budget must appear reasonable to begin with if it is to be useful.

Example

The illustration (Figure 12) is of a profit budget for a seasonal business with a financial year running from October to September, split into periods of four or five weeks, the number of weeks being indicated at the top of the column for each month.

Sales for the year have been estimated at £84,000, and the allocation to each month worked out using last year as a guide. That is, if £84,000 represents an increase of 10% on last year's takings, then the allocation to each month may be taken as 10% more than the same period last year, allowing for any differences in the number of weeks, incidence of Easter or other special factors.

Gross profit is estimated at 60% of sales for each month and the year's total.

Wages and salaries are estimated on the basis of approximately 30% of sales, but unlike gross profit, the cost of employing staff is not directly proportionate to sales. Overtime due to an unexpected rush can cause increased wages cost without an overall increase in takings, and takings themselves can fluctuate within certain limits without altering wages. The forecasts for each period have therefore been estimated only to the nearest £50, taking into account the season of the year and how many weeks in each period rather than small fluctuations in takings. October and November are both four-week periods, but the budget for wages in October is higher than for November on the assumption that summer staff would be run down in October, while November wages would be only for permanent staff.

Fixed expenses are estimated to amount to £8,320 for the year, including rent, rates, insurance, and depreciation. This amounts to £160 per week, which is £640 for a four-week period or £800 for a five-week period.

PROFIT BUDGET 19__/19__

Month	Oct	Nov	Dec	Jan	Feb	Mar	April	May	June	July	Aug	Sept	Total
No. of weeks	4	4	5	4	4	5	4	4	5	4	4	5	52
Sales	5,400	4,800	6,000	4,800	4,200	6,000	5,400	6,000	8,400	11,400	13,200	8,400	84,000
Gross profit	3,240	2,880	3,600	2,880	2,520	3,600	3,240	3,600	5,040	6,840	7,920	5,040	50,400
Wages and salaries	1,800	1,400	1,800	1,400	1,400	1,800	1,800	1,800	2,400	3,400	3,800	2,400	26,200
Fixed expenses	640	640	800	640	640	800	640	640	800	640	640	800	8,320
Variable expenses	400	360	440	360	360	440	400	520	600	720	880	600	6,080
	2,840	2,400	3,040	2,400	2,400	3,040	2,840	2,960	3,800	4,760	5,320	3,800	39,600
Net profit	400	480	560	480	120	560	400	640	1,240	2,080	2,600	1,240	10,800

Figure 12. A profit budget

Variable expenses in this case are taken at about $7\frac{1}{2}\%$ of takings, but again using last year as a guide, and not trying to estimate too exactly. The expenses shown in the illustration have been summarized in order to simplify the explanation. In practice, it would be better to detail each item of expense such as repairs, renewals, lighting and heating, telephone, advertising, and so on.

All expenses are then added up, and the totals deducted from gross profit to find the net profit for each month and the year as a whole. At this stage, wishes and intentions concerning the achieving of net profit for next year may cause hurried revision of ideas about certain estimates already entered. What looks right for each month separately may look very wrong for the year as a whole, and vice versa. A little adjusting, however, should produce a budget statement which represents a reasonable view of next year's probable results. More important, it provides a yardstick with which to compare next year's results as they occur.

Example

From the following information prepare a budget statement for the year ending 28 February 19.. and for each quarter.

Sales last year amounted to £59,728, and for the coming year are to be estimated at $12\frac{1}{2}\%$ above last year (to the nearest £100). Sales vary during the year, the amounts for the quarters to May, August, November, and February being in the ratio 3:5: 4:2.

Gross profit is estimated at 60% of sales.

Wages are estimated at 32% of sales.

Fixed expenses amount to £5,200 p.a.

Variable expenses are estimated at 9% of sales.

Show on your budget statement the net profit percentages on sales for each quarter and the year.

Answer

BUDGET STATEMENT FOR 19../19..

	May	Aug.	Nov.	Feb.	Year
Sales	14,400	24,000	19,200	9,600	67,200
Gross profit	8,640	14,400	11,520	5,760	40,320

Wages	4,608	7,680	6,144	3,072	21,504
Fixed expenses	1,300	1,300	1,300	1,300	5,200
Variable expenses	1,296	2,160	1,728	864	6,048
	7,204	11,140	9,172	5,236	32,752
Net profit	1,436	3,260	2,348	524	7,568
Net profit %	10·0%	13·6%	12·2%	5·5%	11·3%

EXERCISES

1. Describe how you would prepare a monthly estimated profit and loss account stating briefly how the figures are obtained.

(H.C.I.M.A.)

2. The annual costs of The Gourmet Restaurant are:

	£
Rent and rates	1,200
Wages	5,400
Replacements of utensils, etc.	240
Depreciation of fixed assets	360

In addition to the above, fuel costs are 10% of the cost of food. Sales average £15,000 p.a., and the monthly figures vary according to season. Prices shown on the menu are arrived at by taking the cost of the food plus 150%.

You are required to:

(a) Calculate the estimated annual profit.

(b) Prepare an estimate of cost and profit for next month, assuming an estimated sales of £1,500.

(H.C.I.M.A.)

3. Budgets for the coming year are required by the Robin Restaurant, and you ascertain the following information:

Sales last year amounted to £23,204, and it is estimated that sales for the coming year will be 10% more than last year (to the nearest £100). Budgets are to be prepared for the year and for each quarter, ending in March, June, September, and December. Sales in the September quarter account for 40% of a year's sales, in the June quarter 30% of the total, and in the other two quarters sales are about equal.

Gross profit is to be estimated at 60% of sales.

Labour cost is to be estimated at 20% of sales throughout the year.

Fixed expenses amount to £3,000 for the year.

Variable expenses are to be estimated at 15% of sales (to the nearest £5).

Show on your budget statement the net profit percentage of sales for each quarter and for the year.

4. The Nouveau Restaurant has a maximum capacity of 160 customers per day, and is open on 364 days in a year. For the coming year it is estimated that business will average 70% of capacity, but in January business will be 40%. The average price of meals sold will be £3·00. Labour cost is expected to be 25% of takings, variable expenses 15%, food cost 40%, and fixed expenses £12,000. Prepare a statement showing the estimated net profit for the year, and for the four weeks ending 28 January.

16. Cash Budgets

ANY financial estimates for the future will sooner or later require an estimate of the cash available, and a budget statement for this can be systematically built up in a way very similar to a profit budget, and indeed using many of the same figures. The object is to forecast what cash will be available at different times throughout the coming year, so that plans can be made to incur unusual expenditure at a convenient time, to avoid an unnecessarily high overdraft by spreading payments, to arrange additional finance if needed, or even to place surplus cash on deposit instead of leaving it in a current account. Normally the time intervals used will be months or periods of four or five weeks if this method has been used for the purposes of a profit budget, and a typical cash budget will contain forecasts of money to be received and paid for each of twelve periods.

In preparing a cash budget it must be remembered all the time that it is the *cash* position that we are concerned with, and the estimates entered for each month should be the amounts we expect to receive or pay *in that month*. We are not concerned here with profitability, or whether any amount relates to the month, but simply: did it affect our bank balance in that month? For this reason capital items, which were ignored in estimating profit, will have to be allowed for, if they involve movement of cash. Expenses paid in cash will be allowed for in both budgets, but in different months if credit is taken, so that the actual payment is later than the month to which it relates.

Figure 13 illustrates a suitable ruling for a cash budget in a business with a financial year ending on 31 March. The months are written along the top and the descriptions of receipts and payments down the side. These descriptions should be chosen to suit the business, but it is a good plan always to include 'sundries' or 'miscellaneous' as one heading so that space can be found to insert items not conveniently included under other headings.

Having ruled up the statement the first item to consider will naturally be takings, and if we have prepared a profit budget we shall start with the takings estimated for that purpose. It is useless to make different estimates of the same thing just because they are

	April	May	June	July	Aug.	Sept.	Oct.	Nov.	Dec.	Jan.	Feb.	Mar.
Receipts												
Takings												
Miscellaneous												
Payments												
Purchases												
Wages, Salaries, and Nat. Ins.												
P.A.Y.E. and Grad. Pension												
Rates												
Insurance												
Gas and Electricity												
Fuel												
Renewals												
Maintenance												
Advertising												
Postage, Printing and Stationery												
Bank charges												
Sundry expenses												
Capital expenditure												
Taxation												
....												
....												
Surplus/Deficit for the month												
Balance brought forward												
Balance carried forward												

Cash budget 19__ / 19__

Figure 13. A cash budget

required for different purposes. The only question to consider is whether the total sales will be received in cash and in the same month. It may be that the incidence of cash discount will reduce the cash actually received, and credit terms may result in the takings for March being actually received in April.

Similar reasoning will apply to the estimates of payments for purchases. The amount of the cost *for* each month can be taken from the profit budgets, and the amount to be paid *in* each month worked out from that. It follows that where one month's credit is taken, the cost for the months March to February will be required to find the payments in the months April to March, and if cash discount is taken, the payment will be that much less.

Wages will be paid in the month to which they relate, except perhaps for the last week in a month if there is a time lag between pay week and pay day. This can be adjusted for, but is not considered necessary since to take into account a wages payment a little early is to err on the side of prudence. The payments themselves, however, will not be the same amount as the wages for the month because of deductions for P.A.Y.E. and Contributions to National Insurance. These will be paid a month later than the period to which they relate and should be entered accordingly.

Fixed expenses such as rates and insurance will have been apportioned to each month in the profit budget, but the actual payments will be made only once or twice each year, and must be entered on the cash budget when they are paid.

In this way all the expected payments in the coming year can gradually be entered, including all the revenue payments and tax payments which would not be included in a calculation of profit. Note that depreciation will be included in the profit budget, but should be ignored in preparing the cash budget. It is an expense, but it is not paid in cash. It reduces the value of equipment, but does not affect the bank balance, with which the cash budget is concerned.

Example

In Chapter 15 we prepared a profit budget and we can now prepare a cash budget from the same forecasts, plus the following additional information:

1. 80% of Sales are received in the same month, 20% are received in the following month.
2. Purchases are made on one month's credit. No discount.

3. Wages paid in the same month. Ignore P.A.Y.E. adjustment.
4. Fixed charges (£8,320) are made up as follows:
    Rent £4,000 p.a. paid quarterly on usual quarter days.
    Rates £1,624 p.a. paid half-yearly in October and April.
    Insurance £336 p.a. paid annually in January.
    Depreciation £2,360 p.a.
5. Income Tax £4,200 is payable in January.
6. A repayment of investment £1,000 is receivable in January.
7. The cash balance on 1 October 19. . is £2,840.
8. Purchases for September 19. . are £3,200, and Sales are £7,200.
9. Capital expenditure £2,400 is to be paid in March.

The completed cash budget is given in Figure 14 and should be prepared as follows:

1. Receipts from Sales are best entered on two lines showing 80% of each month's sales as received in the same month, 20% in the following month. In October, £1,440 will be received as 20% of September sales £7,200.

2. *Sundry receipts* will consist of the repayments of investment expected to be received in January.

3. *Purchases* for each month can be estimated from the profit budget by deducting estimated gross profit from estimated sales. These purchases will be payable in the following month since they are made on one month's credit.

Purchases *paid for* in October are purchases *for* September, which are not shown on the profit budget beginning in October, so the amount is given as additional information (from the profit budget for the previous year).

Purchases for October amount to £2,160, calculated from the profit budget (sales £5,400 less gross profit £3,240), and this amount is entered on the cash budget for November.

4. *Wages* to be paid each month will be the amounts already estimated for the profit budget.

5. *Fixed expenses* need completely different treatment in the cash budget from that used in the profit budget, although the estimated annual amounts are the same for both purposes. The total of fixed expenses in the profit budget includes depreciation which must be excluded from the cash budget because it does not involve any payment in cash. The other items such as rent and rates are paid in cash, but at different times, and each one must be entered according to the time and amount of payments made.

CASH BUDGET 19__/19__

	Oct.	Nov.	Dec.	Jan.	Feb.	Mar.	April.	May.	June.	July.	Aug.	Sept.
Receipts												
Sales – Cash	4,320	3,840	4,800	3,840	3,360	4,800	4,320	4,800	6,720	9,120	10,560	6,720
Credit	1,440	1,080	960	1,200	960	840	1,200	1,080	1,200	1,680	2,280	2,640
Sundry receipts				1,000								
	5,760	4,920	5,760	6,040	4,320	5,640	5,520	5,880	7,920	10,800	12,840	9,360
Payments												
Purchases	3,200	2,160	1,920	2,400	1,920	1,680	2,400	2,160	2,400	3,360	4,560	5,280
Wages	1,800	1,400	1,800	1,400	1,400	1,800	1,800	1,800	2,400	3,400	3,800	2,400
Rent			1,000			1,000			1,000			1,000
Rates	812						812					
Insurance				336								
Expenses	400	360	440	360	360	440	400	520	600	720	880	600
Capital expenditure				4,200								
Taxation						2,400						
	6,212	3,920	5,160	8,696	3,680	7,320	5,412	4,480	6,400	7,480	9,240	9,280
Increase (Reduction) in cash	(452)	1,000	600	(2,656)	640	(1,680)	108	1,400	1,520	3,320	3,600	80
Balance from last month	2,840	2,388	3,388	3,988	1,332	1,972	292	400	1,800	3,320	6,640	10,240
Balance carried forward	2,388	3,388	3,988	1,332	1,972	292	400	1,800	3,320	6,640	10,240	10,320

Figure 14. Completed cash budget

6. *Variable expenses* in this example are assumed to be paid when they are incurred and are entered in the same month as in the profit budget.

7. *Capital expenditure* does not appear in the profit budget, but we know that £2,400 is expected to be paid in March, and this must be entered on the cash budget.

8. *Taxation*, like capital expenditure, must be entered on the cash budget although it did not appear on the profit budget.

9. *Total receipts and total payments* should now be entered.

10. *Increase (Reduction) in cash* is found by deducting total payments from total receipts in each month. If total receipts are greater than total payments in any month, then that month has produced a surplus which will increase the balance of cash at the bank. If total payments are greater than total receipts there is a deficit which will reduce the balance. It is convenient to identify a reduction by marking it in some way or by entering it in red ink. In the illustration reductions are shown in brackets.

11. *Balance from last month* is the balance carried forward in the previous month. The balance from September this year, with which October will be started, is £2,840 and this should be entered in the October column. The figure immediately above shows a reduction of £452 for the month of October which should be deducted from the £2,840 balance at 1 October, and the balance at the end of October £2,388 entered as 'balance carried forward'. This amount can immediately be entered as the 'balance from last month' in November, and when added to the surplus £1,000 in November gives a £3,388 balance carried forward. This is then entered in December, and so on throughout the year.

In this example the payment of £2,400 for capital expenditure was assumed to be payable in March, but the time of payment for this kind of item will probably be discretionary. In that case the cash budget would be completed without any entry for capital expenditure, so that the position can be seen, and the best time for this payment can be chosen. It will be seen that if an entry had been made for this £2,400 payment in any month before March, a bank overdraft would have resulted. March is the earliest date when it could be paid without causing an overdraft, and if this date is otherwise suitable (e.g. in time for the season), plans would be made accordingly.

It should always be borne in mind that a budget is a forecast of what is likely to happen in the future and, in consequence, is liable to error. As each month goes by the actual figures for the month can be substituted for the estimated figures and the forecast for the rest of the year becomes that much more certain. For this purpose it is helpful to prepare the original budget statement in pencil and to ink in actual figures as they occur. In the above example, at the end of October this year it may be found that the actual receipts and payments, which would be inked in on the statement, looked like this:

	£
Total receipts	5,656
Payments:	
Purchases	3,136
Wages	1,888
Rates	812
Expenses	316
	£6,152
Increase (Reduction) in cash	(496)
Balance from last month	2,840
Balance carried forward	£2,344

The balance at the end of October is now seen to be £2,344, instead of the forecast £2,388, and the forecast balances for the rest of the year can be amended in pencil accordingly. Similarly at the end of November another set of actual figures can be inked in and amended balances pencilled in for the rest of the year. In making these amendments, it may be noticed that certain items have been consistently over- or underestimated, and it may be thought advisable to alter the estimates of these items for the rest of the year, further amending the balances. In this way the budget becomes more and more accurate as each month goes by, and at the end of the year provides a good basis on which to estimate next year's forecasts.

EXERCISES

1. Explain what is meant by a cash budget and in what important respects it differs from a profit budget.
2. The sales of a restaurant consist entirely of cash takings, but all

purchases are on monthly credit terms. From the following information, find out how much the net increase or reduction in the bank balance will be, with respect to sales and purchases, for each of the months July, August, and September:

	Purchases £	Sales £
Purchases and sales *for* May	600	1,500
June	800	2,000
July	1,000	2,500
August	1,800	4,500
September	600	1,500

3. The purchases of a restaurant are subject to one month's credit, and payment made less a deduction of $2\frac{1}{2}\%$ cash discount. If the purchases for June, July, August, and September are expected to be respectively £680, £1,240, £1,760, and £1,320, what amounts should be taken into the cash budget statement, and in which months should they be entered?

4. From the following information prepare a cash budget for the months of June, July, August, and September, 19..:

	£
1 June 19.. Bank balance	51,269
Sales for April	31,465
Sales for May	29,658
Estimated sales for June	42,147
Estimated sales for July	58,393
Estimated sales for August	61,215
Estimated sales for September	52,147

Investment income due 30 June 19..
£1,000 – receivable in July.

Estimated expenses for June (including wages and salaries)	10,213
Estimated expenses for July	10,869
Estimated expenses for August	11,019
Estimated expenses for September	10,542

Purchases for May	49,251
Estimated purchases for June	52,375
Estimated purchases for July	19,142

Estimated purchases August   11,641
Estimated purchases for September   16,842

Rent payable on 30 June 19..   1,200
Rent payable on 30 September 19..   1,200

Interim dividend of 5% on capital of
£50,000 payable on 1 July 19..

Allow for two months' credit on sales.
Allow for one month's credit on purchases.

Discuss briefly the use of such a cash budget.

(H.C.I.M.A)

5. Discuss the purposes and advantages of a cash budget and prepare
   such a budget for the months of July, August, and September 19..,
   based on the following information:

		£
Bank and cash balance at 1 July		23,609
Sales for May		18,405
Estimated sales for June		19,811
	July	15,402
	August	17,663
Purchases for May		4,976
Estimated purchases for June		5,086
	July	5,023
	August	4,982
Estimated expenses payable in July		3,842
	August	4,185
	September	3,976

One quarter's rent at £3,600 p.a.
payable on 1 July.
Half year's rates at £1,200 p.a.
payable on 1 July.
Interim dividend of 5% on capital of
£60,000 due to be paid 2 July (ignore
taxation).

Investment income expected 5 July		2,000
Estimated wages to be paid in July		4,061
	August	5,004
	September	3,896

Sales accounts are settled on average six weeks after the end of the month in which sales were made.

Purchase accounts are settled on the 20th of the month following the end of the month in which the purchases were made.

(H.C.I.M.A.)

17. *Daily Cash Budgets*

HAVING prepared a cash budget for each month of the year it may be useful to have detailed information of what is likely to happen at different times within each month. For example the cash budget in Figure 14 shows that a balance of only £292 is expected at the end of March. It cannot be seen from the budget statement whether the balance is expected to come down to this figure early in March and stay there most of the month, or whether the balance should be higher for most of the month, and be reduced by payments only at the end. Indeed, it could be that most of the payments would be made early, and receipts received late, so that there would be an overdraft during March which was corrected only at the end. Since an overdraft costs money in interest, it would be foolish to incur this expense if it could be avoided, which means planning on a day-to-day basis.

Example

Taking the facts for March in the cash budget shown at Figure 14 assume the five-week period commences on Sunday, 1 March, and ends on Saturday, 4 April, and that the takings in the month are expected to be received proportionately each week. A daily cash budget would be prepared in advance, in pencil as before, for inking in when the actual figures become known. There should be provision for showing the balance at the beginning of the period covered, amounts received and amounts paid, and the balance after each day's transactions.

In practice, if the working week is taken to end on Saturday night, the takings for the week will not be banked on the Saturday but on the following Monday, so for practical purposes the daily cash budget for the March period will run from the balance after the banking on 2 March until after the banking on 6 April.

A daily cash budget prepared on this basis is shown at Figure 15, and it will be seen that the £2,400 capital expenditure could not be paid earlier than 6 April without making the balance overdrawn. This can now be planned ahead.

If wages are to be paid out of cash takings, and only the net amount banked, then the daily cash budget would be prepared accordingly. Similarly, the cash budget for March in respect of salaries and wages may include weekly wages and salaries paid at the end of the month, which would be shown on the daily cash budget.

DAILY CASH BUDGET

Date		Receipts	Payments	Balance
March 2	Balance			1,972
7	Expenses		88	
7	Wages		360	1,524
9	Takings	840		2,364
14	Expenses		88	
14	Wages		360	1,916
16	Takings	1,200		
16	February Creditors		1,680	1,436
21	Expenses		88	
21	Wages		360	988
23	Takings	1,200		2,188
25	Rent		1,000	
28	Expenses		88	
28	Wages		360	740
30	Takings	1,200		1,940
April 4	Expenses		88	
4	Wages		360	1,492
6	Takings	1,200		2,692
6	Capital Expenditure		2,400	292

Remarks:

Figure 15. Daily cash budget

The daily cash budget for each month will start with the balance at the end of the previous month, which will still be only a forecast figure at the time it is prepared. However, at the end of the previous month the actual balance can be inked in and any adjustments made to the budget for the coming month.

In considering the daily cash budget for March we were concerned to avoid running into an overdraft. It may be, however, that the bank balance is high enough for this to be no problem, in which case the question immediately arises: is too much being kept in the bank current account? If a greater balance is kept on current account than is needed for current commitments, then interest is being lost, which could otherwise be earned by placing the surplus on deposit account. To do 'his to full advantage, however, needs careful forward planning, particularly with regard to timing of withdrawl again from deposit account. The normal seven days' notice will be required if full interest is to be obtained, and preparation of a daily cash budget will enable this to be planned at the right time.

Example

The main cash budget for June (Figure 14) shows that we expect to begin the month with a balance of £1,800 and end with a balance of £3,320. If it is considered that about £100 must be kept for emergencies, and that anything more than that could be placed on deposit, the first step in planning will be to prepare the daily cash budget. We will assume that takings for last month £1,200 are received in the first

DAILY CASH BUDGET				
Date		Receipts	Payments	Balance
June 1	Balance			1,800
7	Takings less wages etc	600		2,400
14	Net Takings	1,080		
14	Creditors		2,400	1,080
21	Net takings	1,080		2,160
24	Rent		1,000	1,160
28	Net takings	1,080		2,240
July 5	Net takings	1,080		3,320

Figure 16. Draft daily cash budget

week, remaining takings being spread over four weeks. Wages £2,400 and Expenses £600 divided by five (£600) are deducted from bankings each week; if we had reason to expect the weekly proportions to be different, we would budget accordingly. A draft would first be prepared without any transfer to deposit (Figure 16).

Now we could put £1,700 on deposit on 1 June, and a further £600 on 7 June, but at the same time on 7 June we must give notice of withdrawal on 14 June of £1,300 to be transferred back to the current account to meet the payment of creditors. These transfers can be adjusted on the daily cash budget as we think of them so that the picture is kept up to date. At this stage the pencil figures would look like those in Figure 17.

DAILY CASH BUDGET					
Date		Receipts	Payments	Balance	
				C/A	Deposit
June 1	Balance			1,800	
1	Transfer to deposit		1,700	100	1,700
* 7	Net takings	600			
7	Transfer to deposit		600	100	2,300
14	Net takings	1,080			
14	Transfer from deposit	1,300			1,000
14	Creditors		2,400	80	
21	Net takings	1,080		1,160	
24	Rent		1,000	160	
28	Net takings	1,080		1,240	
July 5	Net takings	1,080		2,320	

Figure 17. Daily cash budget: second stage

Putting an asterisk alongside the date at 7 June will remind us that notice must be given to withdraw £1,300 from deposit account the following week.

As the budget now stands it appears that the need to pay rent on 24 June will stop us from transferring any more cash to deposit until 28 June, when we could transfer another £1,100. In order to decide what we should do on 5 July we must obtain some idea of what the position will be in July. In other words, prepare a daily cash budget for July following on from that for June. We will assume that this shows no need for withdrawal from deposit early in the month, so that another £1,100 could be put to deposit on 5 July. The final budget will be as Figure 18.

The cash balance at 5 July will still be £3,320, as shown on the main cash budget, but it will be divided between two accounts. The interest earned by this manœuvring will amount to about £50 in this example for the months June to September at no risk, without much trouble, and on comparatively small figures. There is no risk because

DAILY CASH BUDGET

Date		Receipts	Payments	Balance C/A	Deposit
June 1	Balance			1,800	
1	Transfer to deposit		1,700	100	1,700
* 7	Net takings	600			
7	Transfer to deposit		600	100	2,300
14	Net takings	1,080			
14	Transfer from deposit	1,300			1,000
14	Creditors		2,400	80	
21	Net takings	1,080		1,160	
24	Rent		1,000	160	
28	Net takings	1,080			
28	Transfer to deposit		1,100	140	2,100
July 5	Net takings	1,080			
6	Transfer to deposit		1,100	120	3,200

Remarks:

* Give notice of withdrawal to bank

Figure 18. Final daily cash budget

the money on deposit will always be available for emergency even if proper notice of withdrawal cannot be given. The effect of giving seven days' notice is to avoid losing a little interest, which is credited up to the date of withdrawal if proper notice is given. If the withdrawal is required at less than seven days' notice, some interest will be forfeited, but the sum actually on deposit will be available when required. It is not unobtainable in a hurry as is the case with some investments.

It is convenient to note the balance on deposit alongside the current account balance on the daily cash budget, so that the overall position can be easily seen. It is usually sufficient to enter the deposit balance only when a change has been made, the balance at any time being the last amount entered. Thus in Figure 17 the balance on deposit at 5 July is £1,000. This was the balance remaining after transferring £1,300 to current account on 14 June, and will still be the balance, since there have been no further transfers to or from the deposit account.

EXERCISES

1. Briefly explain the advantages to be gained from a daily cash budget and why they cannot be gained from a budget prepared on a monthly basis.

2. The Haven Hotel has a balance of cash at the bank amounting to £874 on 1 April, and the cash budget for the four weeks ending 28 April is as follows:

	£
Receipts	3,300
Payments	
Purchases for March	1,440
Wages	850
Expenses	120
	2,410
Net surplus for the month	890
Balance brought forward	874
Balance carried forward	£1,764

It is expected that the takings for the last week of the period will be £1,500, and the other three weeks will be evenly spread. Wages for the last week are expected to be £50 more than each of the other weeks, but expenses will be about the same each week.

Prepare a daily cash budget for April, assuming that all the creditors for March purchases will be paid together at the earliest time without causing an overdraft.

3. Briefly explain the relative advantages of earning cash discount at the expense of a bank overdraft, or keeping a credit balance at the bank at the expense of losing cash discounts.

4. The Hive Restaurant has a balance on current account at the bank amounting to £1,500 at 1 July. Cash takings are expected to be £800 for each of the four weeks ending 28 July and wages paid will be £200 each week. Creditors amounting to £1,800 must be paid on 10 July and salaries amounting to £180 on 28 July. What is the earliest date on which £1,000 can be placed on deposit account, and yet retain a balance of at least £500 on current account throughout the month? Illustrate your answer by preparing a daily cash budget.

18. *Cash Flow Statements*

A CASH FLOW STATEMENT is a financial statement summarizing the flow of cash in and out over a period of time, usually a year, and showing its effect on the cash balance. It is in effect an annual summary of the monthly cash budgets, showing the estimated annual totals of receipts and payments, the surplus or deficit for the year, the balance at the beginning of the year, and the estimated balance at the end.

If cash budgets for the year have already been prepared, as in Figure 14, a cash flow statement presents no problem. It is simply a matter of summarizing as follows:

CASH FLOW STATEMENT
YEAR 19../19..

	£	
Receipts		
Sales	83,760	
Sundry receipts	1,000	
		84,760
Payments		
Purchases	33,440	
Wages	25,200	
Rent	4,000	
Rates	1,624	
Insurance	336	
Expenses	6,080	
Capital expenditure	2,400	
Taxation	4,200	
		77,280
Surplus for the year		7,480
Bank balance at 1 October this year		2,840
Forecast bank balance at 30 September next year		£10,320

If cash budgets have not previously been prepared, estimated figures will need to be arrived at for the cash flow statement in much the same way as for cash budget, using annual totals only.

An alternative method of preparing a cash flow statement is to start by adding to the balance at the beginning of the year the forecast profit shown by the profit budget. This assumes that if a profit is made the cash balance will rise. As this is not entirely true because of such items as depreciation and capital expenditure, further adjustment should be made for such items, and the resultant balance will be the forecast bank balance at the end of the year.

CASH FLOW STATEMENT

YEAR 19../19..

Balance at 1 October this year		2,840
Add Profit for year per budget		10,800
		13,640
Add Repayment of investment	1,000	
Depreciation charged	2,360	
Increase in creditors	160	
		3,520
		17,160
Less Capital expenditure	2,400	
Taxation	4,200	
Increase in debtors	240	
		6,840
Forecast balance at 30 September next year		£10,320

The result comes to the same amount whichever method is adopted, but it might be useful to look more closely at the adjustments made in this second method.

1. *Repayment of investment* is added because it represents cash to be received which is not taken into account in the profit budget. As a capital sum it does not form part of the profit for the year, but it will increase the cash balance.

2. *Depreciation* is added because it has been charged against the profit, but has not been paid in cash. The cash profit will therefore be that much more, and the cash balance will be increased by that much more than the net profit.

3. *Increase in creditors* is added because the expenses charged against the profit are the amounts due for the year, not the amounts paid in the year. The amounts paid in the year, which need to be taken into account in a cash flow statement will be the expense for the year, *plus* the creditors at the beginning of the year, *less* the creditors at the end of the year. Creditors at the beginning are added because they will be paid in the year in addition to the expenses for the year. Creditors at the end are deducted because they represent expenses for the year which have not yet paid. The net effect is that expenses actually paid are less than expenses for the year by any increase in creditors, and more by any reduction in creditors. In this example the creditors at 1 October this year were £3,200 (paid in October) and creditors at 30 September next year were £3,360 (the profit budget shows purchases for September next year = sales £8,400 less gross profit £5,040). The increase of £160 represents expenses charged against the profit which will not be paid in the year, and will not therefore reduce the balance. So the balance should be increased by that much more than the profit.

4. *Capital expenditure and taxation* are both items which will reduce the balance but which are not taken care of in the calculation of profit, and must therefore be deducted separately.

5. *Increase in debtors* (£1,440 in October, £1,680 next September) represents sales cash not received in the year.

Example

The financial year of the Quality Restaurant ends on 28 February.
Sales for the financial year are estimated at £40,000.
Cost of food is estimated at 40% of sales.
Labour cost is estimated at 30% of sales.
Rent payable will be £1,800 p.a., rates are £650 p.a., and insurance premiums amount to £113 p.a.
Depreciation at 10% p.a. must be provided on equipment £7,000.
Variable expenses are estimated at 11% of sales.
Sundry creditors at 28 February this year amounted to £13,000 and it is estimated that creditors at 28 February next year will total £5,000.
Equipment to be purchased during the financial year will cost £1,500.
Income Tax £1,712 is payable on 1 January.
The opening bank balance at 1 March is £6,940.
Prepare an estimated profit statement, and a cash flow statement, for the financial year.

Answer

ESTIMATED PROFIT STATEMENT 19../19..

		£
Sales		40,000
Food cost (40% of £40,000)		16,000
Gross profit		24,000
Labour cost (30% of £40,000)		12,000
Overheads		
Rent	1,800	
Rates	650	
Insurance	113	
Depreciation (10% of £7,000)	700	
Variable expenses (11% of £40,000)	4,400	
		7,663
		19,663
Net profit		£4,337

ESTIMATED CASH FLOW STATEMENT 19../19..

		£
Net profit per estimated profit statement		4,337
Add Depreciation		700
		5,037
Less		
Tax	1,712	
Reduction in creditors	8,000	
Capital expenditure	1,500	
		11,212
Excess expenditure for the year		6,175
Bank balance at 1 March this year		6,940
Estimated bank balance at 28 February next year		£ 765

As an explanation of the flow of cash for a period, a cash flow statement may be prepared as a forecast for next year, as in this example, or may be prepared for last year. In this case it reconciles the cash balances at the beginning and end of the year, and relates the cash balances to the other balance sheet items.

Example

From the following balance sheet prepare a cash flow statement for the year ended 31 December 19..

BALANCE SHEET AS AT 31ST DECEMBER 19..

	Last Year £	This Year £
Fixed Assets, at cost	58,000	63,000
less Depreciation	1,900	2,800
	56,100	60,200
Stock	700	800
Debtors	2,100	1,900
Cash	1,300	2,100
	4,100	4,800
Less Creditors	2,700	2,000
	1,400	2,800
Capital Employed	£57,500	£63,000
Capital – balance at 1 Jan	58,200	57,500
Add Profit for the year	4,300	5,300
	62,500	62,800
Less Drawings	5,000	4,800
	57,500	58,000
Loan	—	5,000
	£57,500	£63,000

Answer

CASH FLOW STATEMENT FOR THE YEAR TO 31.12. –

Sources of Cash		£
Net Profit		5,300
Add Depreciation charged		900
		6,200
Reduction in Debtors		200
Loan received		5,000
		11,400

Applications of Cash		
Increase in Stock	100	
Reduction in Creditors	700	
Purchase of fixed Assets	5,000	
Drawings	4,800	
		10,600
Increase in Cash during the year		£ 800

EXERCISES

1. What do you understand by a cash flow statement? Briefly explain one method of preparing such a statement.
2. Briefly explain why the bank balance of a business does not increase by the amount of net profit made. Give three examples of items which will account for the difference.
3. The forecast net profit of the Apex Hotel for the coming year is £5,824 and you obtain the following information:
   The forecast balance of cash at bank at 1 January is £1,138.
   Debtors at 1 January are £314.
   Creditors at 1 January are £1,875.
   Debtors at 31 December will be about the same as in January, but creditors are likely to be £1,000 more.
   Due to alterations to the cellars, it is expected that the bar stocks at 31 December will be £500 more than on 1 January.

Depreciation £650 has been allowed for in calculating the net profit.

Prepare a cash flow statement showing the movement of cash in the coming year and the foreeast cash balance at the end of the year.

4. Prepare a cash flow statement for the year ended 30 September 1980 from the following information:

	1979 £	1980 £
Fixed Assets, at cost	22,800	23,800
Additions	1,000	3,200
	23,800	27,000
less Depreciation	4,600	6,400
	19,200	20,600
Current Assets		
Stock	800	600
Debtors	1,100	1,200
Cash	2,300	2,500
	4,200	4,300
Less Current Liabilities	3,100	2,800
Working Capital	1,100	1,500
	£20,300	£22,100
Capital – balance as last year	19,200	20,300
add Profit	5,100	5,800
	24,300	26,100
less Drawings	4,000	4,000
	£20,300	£22,100

19. *Operating Statements*

A REGULAR statement of costs and profits showing actual results compared with budgets is generally referred to as an *operating statement*. It may show income and costs in considerable detail for the actual accounting period of four or five weeks, and the accumulated amounts for the period from the beginning of the financial year to date. The forecast figures for the year may also be shown, and each item expressed as a percentage of sales (*see* Figure 19).

In the illustration there are five main columns headed Actual for month, Forecast for month, Actual to date, Forecast to date, and Forecast for year. In each main column there is provision for an amount in pounds and a percentage. Down the left-hand side of the page are listed the headings of income and cost, ending with net profit, against each item being shown the actual results compared with the amounts forecast on the budget statement.

Each of the four items of sales is shown as an amount and as a percentage of total sales. It may be thought that the food sales shown are an unusually small proportion of total sales, though the management evidently expected this proportion since the budget figures show the same percentage as the actual figures. It might be instructive to consider what sort of hotel might have a sales mix of this kind.

Cost of sales is not shown on the statement, since it constitutes only the difference between sales and gross profit, and its inclusion would add to an already over-detailed statement. This question of too much detail is of vital importance if costing information is to aid management instead of dazing them, and we will consider below how the statement may be made more readable.

Gross profit in each case is shown as a percentage of the particular source of income, not as a percentage of total sales. This means that for apartments gross profit is shown as 100%, since there is no cost of sales to deduct. Strictly the terms 'sales' and 'gross profit' are not applicable to accommodation charges, since no buying and selling of goods is involved, but it is convenient to deal with the item in this way. Total gross profit is then expressed as a percentage of total sales, as are all the expenses which follow.

	SURF HAVEN HOTEL LTD Operating Statement							Month _April 19.._ _4_ Weeks		
	Actual for month		Forecast for month		Actual to date		Forecast to date		Forecast for year	
	%	£	%	£	%	£	%	£	%	£
Sales Apartments	46	1,816	46	1,800	49	12,825	50	12,600	48	25,000
Food	40	1,587	40	1,500	40	10,468	40	10,200	42	21,000
Liquor	11	423	11	400	9	2,074	8	1,900	8	4,700
Tobacco	3	102	3	100	2	541	2	500	2	1,200
TOTAL SALES	100	3,928	100	3,800	100	25,908	100	25,200	100	51,900
Gross profit Apartments	100	1,816	100	1,800	100	12,825	100	12,600	100	25,000
Food	52	826	52	780	52	5,450	52	5,350	53	11,100
Liquor	50	213	50	200	50	1,039	50	950	50	2,350
Tobacco	8	8	8	8	8	43	8	40	8	100
TOTAL GROSS PROFIT	73	2,863	73	2,788	75	19,357	75	18,940	74	38,550
Wages, Salaries, and Staff meals	33	1,302	33	1,250	32	8,321	31	7,800	31	16,100
Rates and Water	2	79	2	80	2	598	2	600	2	1,040
Electricity	2	60	2	61	2	441	2	461	2	800
Gas	2	71	2	82	2	463	3	610	2	1,050
Fuel	4	152	4	150	5	1,139	4	1,040	3	1,800
Cleaning	1	29	1	31	1	207	1	230	1	400
Flowers and Decorations	–	6	–	10	–	54	–	75	–	130
Repairs and Renewals	7	274	7	270	7	1,861	7	1,820	7	3,500
Advertising	3	116	3	100	3	802	3	750	3	1,300
Entertainment	1	41	1	40	1	315	1	300	1	520
Commissions	–	5	–	10	–	61	–	75	–	130
Laundry	2	72	2	80	2	507	2	600	2	1,040
Uniforms	–	15	–	10	–	88	–	75	–	130
Printing, Stationery, and Postages	–	8	–	10	–	74	–	75	–	130
Telephone	1	24	1	30	1	189	1	225	1	390
Insurance	1	20	1	20	1	150	1	150	1	260
Licences	–	5	–	5	–	37	–	37	–	60
Motor expenses	1	52	2	60	1	317	2	450	2	780
Miscellaneous expenses	1	31	1	29	1	185	1	210	1	380
Bad debts	–	–	–	9	–	41	–	65	–	120
Bank charges	–	10	–	10	–	75	–	75	–	130
Legal and Professional fees	–	10	–	8	–	42	–	60	–	100
Audit and Accountancy	–	9	–	9	–	71	–	71	–	125
Depreciation	3	130	4	130	4	980	4	980	3	1,700
Directors fees	4	154	4	154	5	1,154	5	1,154	4	2,000
	68	2,675	70	2,648	70	18,172	70	17,988	66	34,115
Discount received	1	21	1	25	–	157	–	166	1	340
NET EXPENSES	67	2,654	69	2,623	70	18,015	70	17,822	65	33,775
NET PROFIT	6	209	4	165	5	1,342	5	1,118	9	4,775

Figure 19. An operating statement

An operating statement for a restaurant would have no entries relating to apartments, but would follow the same pattern and would otherwise look just the same.

INTERPRETATION OF AN
OPERATING STATEMENT

In considering a statement of this kind it is more informative and less bewildering to start with the final result, and afterwards look into the detailed information contributing to this result. The final result in this case is the net profit for the period to date, £1,342, which we are able to compare with the forecast net profit to date, £1,118, and see that the actual result is better than the forecast. This leads naturally to considering the eventual profit for the year, which was forecast at £4,775, and we are able to say at this stage that the trend so far suggests that the actual annual profit may be greater. It is no more than a likelihood so far, which may be reversed in later months, but regular comparison of this kind will obviate the risk of any incipient change in trend from passing unnoticed and unchecked.

From considering the cumulative net profit the next stage is to look at the net profit for the month, £209, compared with the forecast £165. Again the trend appears to be in the same direction, which is satisfactory if the forecast figures have been carefully prepared, and the last thing to note from this bottom line of the operating statement will be the percentages of total sales. First it will be noted that the percentages of figures to date are all lower than the forecast for the year. This immediately suggests a seasonal business, in which the sales in the season increase so much that they easily absorb the overheads and leave a greater proportion of net profit. The net profit in the summer months may thus be 15%, compared with 5% up to April, making the percentage for the year 9%.

If the actual net profit to date is greater than the forecast amount, but both actual and forecast net profits represent 5% of their respective sales, then the actual turnover must be higher than expected. This is so, as will be seen from the top of the statement.

So far the results have appeared to be satisfactory, but examination of the detailed sales figures shows that the actual apartments takings to date are 49% of total takings instead of the 50% forecast, whereas liquor takings are 9% of the total instead of 8%. The effect is not significant at present and apparently occurred before April, since the sales-mix proportions for the month are as forecast. However, it should be borne in mind that apartments takings produce 100% gross profit, whereas liquor takings produce only 50%. So long as the change is caused only by increases in liquor sales, and not by a fall in apartments takings, the result is acceptable, but otherwise it would be a clear indication of falling profits.

The next step is to look at the gross profit figures, which in this case are all as forecast. It sometimes happens that the overall gross profit seems adequate, but the detailed figures show that a poor result on, say, wines is being obscured by the greater food figures.

The main expense to be met out of gross profit is for wages, salaries, and staff meals, and this amount is greater than forecast. We would expect the amount itself to be higher because of the higher turnover, but in this case the *proportion* of turnover is 32% instead of the forecast 31%. However the percentage for the month is 33%, which is exactly as forecast, so the increase occurred earlier in the year and has apparently been rectified. Each of the other items should be examined in the same critical way, looking for signs of any avoidable waste so that the necessary action can be taken. Fuel is another expense which apparently needed looking into earlier in the year, and which is now reduced again to forecast cost.

The method of looking at such a mass of figures has been at each stage to look at the effect, as represented by the total, and then to study the cause, as represented by the detailed figures. To make this task easier it is useful to break the operating statement into parts, comprising a front page with totals only, followed by schedules of detailed figures which can be referred to when required. In this way the mass of figures is seen only when it is being referred to for specific items, and does not produce the familiar effect of not being able to see the wood for the trees.

EXAMINATION QUESTION

Example

The profit budget of the Lunar Restaurant for June contains the following forecasts: sales £3,500 (100%); gross profit £2,100 (60%); wages, salaries, and staff meals £700 (20%); fixed expenses £400 (11%); variable expenses £525 (15%); net profit £475 (14%).

The actual results for June were: sales £4,000; food cost £1,800; wages, salaries, and staff meals £800; fixed expenses £400; variable expenses £600.

Prepare an operating statement for June, showing percentages correct to the nearest whole number. Comment briefly on the results shown.

Answer

LUNAR RESTAURANT

Operating Statement — June 19___

	Actual		Budget	
	%	£	%	£
Sales	100	4,000	100	3,500
Gross profit	55	2,200	60	2,100
Wages, Salaries, and Staff meals	20	800	20	700
Fixed expenses	10	400	11	400
Variable expenses	15	600	15	525
	45	1,800	46	1,625
Net profit	10	400	14	475

Note: Actual net profit is less than the budget net profit in both amount and as a percentage of turnover. This is due to the rate of gross profit being only 55% of turnover instead of 60%, with the result that the amount of gross profit is not sufficient to cover the expenses and the expected rate of net profit. Wages and variable expenses are higher, but remain in proportion to the higher sales.

EXERCISES

1. Briefly explain what you understand by an operating statement and how such a statement can be an aid to management.
2. Give four possible reasons why the actual gross profit percentage of sales may be less than the budget percentage.
3. The following figures are extracted from the books of the Solar Restaurant for the four weeks ending 28 June:
   Food stocks at 1 June £165; food stocks at 28 June £130; food purchases £1,172; sales £3,078; wages, salaries, and staff meals £921; overheads £770.
   The budget figures for the month were:
   Sales £2,700; gross profit £1,620; wages, salaries, and staff meals £675; overheads £675; net profit £270.
   (a) Prepare an operating statement for the month, showing percentages correct to the nearest whole number.
   (b) Comment briefly on the results, drawing attention to any item that you think requires investigation.

4. Prepare an operating statement for the Apex Hotel, using the following information and showing percentages correct to the nearest whole number. Figures for April (budgets in brackets): apartments takings £6,147 (£6,000); food takings £9,681 (£9,000); wines takings £872 (£1,000); food gross profit £5,755 (£5,400); wines gross profit £440 (£500); labour cost £3,173 (£3,200); overheads £6,714 (£6,900).

If the present trend continues throughout the year, is the forecast net profit for the year overestimated, underestimated, or about right?

5. The Manor Hotel has sixty beds available nightly and provides food only to guests. It has no licence. Rooms are charged at £1·50 per night, food being charged separately, You are required to prepare an operating statement for April, showing the results of apartments and food separately, from the following information:

	Actual £	Budget £
Takings:		
Apartments	1,620	1,500
Food	2,430	2,300
Cost of food	1,142	1,035 (45%)
Wages:		
Apartments	500	450 (30%)
Food	600	575 (25%)
Fixed expenses:		
Apartments	150	150 (10%)
Food	230	230 (10%)
Variable expenses:		
Apartments	730	675 (45%)
Food	125	115 (5%)

Show against each item of actual cost the percentage of the appropriate sales figure, and note the occupancy rate achieved for the month (thirty days).

20. Marginal Costing

IF a hotel sells 20,000 bed-nights in a year, and total costs amount to £150,000, then the total cost per bed-night is £7·50. If the average charge is £9·00 per bed-night, a net profit of £1·50 per bed-night is being made, which amounts to £30,000 per year. This may be regarded as the normal business of the hotel, and every sale is expected to bear its due proportion of costs and contribute to net profit.

With all this normal business already completed, if the hotel contemplates selling some extra bed-nights, what is the minimum charge which must be made for the extra business to be profitable? It might be thought that the charge must be more than the cost £7·50, but it should be remembered that this figure includes fixed costs, and there will be no extra fixed costs to be met out of the extra takings. Costs do not all behave in the same way. Some like Rent, Rates, Insurance, remain fixed in amount irrespective of how much business is being done, and are known as Fixed Costs. Some like Food Cost vary in total amount in proportion to the number of sales made, and are known as Variable Costs. Some costs are semi-variable in that they do increase or reduce with changes in business done, but not in proportion. Expenses such as renewals of cutlery and crockery will be heavier if there are many more customers, but possibly no more if there are only a few more customers. The increase cannot be calculated, it can only be estimated from knowledge of the business. After estimating the total increase in semi-variable costs for an increased number of sales, the increased cost per sale can be calculated. It will thus be seen that if we consider the costs of a business at any level of output, the extra cost incurred by producing one more unit will consist of the variable cost per unit plus the increase in semi-variable costs per unit. This is known as the Marginal Cost.

Marginal Cost is defined as 'the increase or reduction in total cost, at a given volume of output, resulting from an increase or reduction of one unit of output'. In other words if we sell one more item our costs will increase by the marginal cost; if we sell one fewer, our costs will go down by the marginal cost. The term Marginal Costing is used to describe the technique of identifying this extra cost of extra output, and providing guidance on whether the extra is worth doing. In other industries, the technique has relevance to the valuation of work-in-progress, but in hotels and catering there are two main applications; considering whether to accept proposed extra business at a reduced tariff, and whether to open in the off-season.

Contribution

The difference between the selling price per unit of additional sales, and the marginal cost of those sales, is the contribution per unit to fixed expenses and profit, generally referred to simply as the Contribution. If the selling price is greater, there will be a contribution to profit from the additional sales. If the marginal cost is greater than the selling price (a negative contribution) the extra business will result in a loss.

In a period when losses are being made due to high fixed expenses, a positive contribution may contribute to the fixed expenses and so reduce the loss, without actually turning the loss into a profit. In this case the additional business is profitable and worth doing despite the overall loss.

Extra Business at Reduced Tariff

If a tour operator proposes a block-booking out of season at a reduced tariff, it will not be immediately apparent whether the extra business will be profitable, particularly if the proposed selling price per person is less than the normal cost per person.

Provided the proposal does not interfere with normal business, what matters is whether there will be a contribution from the extra meals or extra sleeper nights. If so, the total profit will be greater with the extra business than without it. If there is a negative contribution, the total profit will be less if the proposal is adopted than without it.

Example

A hotel sells on average 20,000 bed-nights in a year, and achieves the following results:

	Per Year £	Per Bed-night £
Sales	160,000	8·00
Food Cost	60,000	3·00
Fixed Expenses	26,000	1·30
Variable Expenses	30,000	1·50
Semi-variable Expenses	28,000	1·40
	144,000	7·20
Net Profit	£16,000	£0·80

A tour operator proposes to bring coach parties out of season totalling 400 extra bed-nights at £6·00 per person per night. It is estimated that this would cause an increase of £200 in semi-variable expenses. As the proposed charge £6·00 is less than the cost per person £7·20, should the proposal be rejected?

Answer

The marginal cost of the extra business is £5·00 as follows:

	£
Food Cost	3·00
Variable Expenses	1·50
Semi-variable "(£200 ÷ 400)	0·50
	5·00

Food Cost and Variable Expenses are both variable costs, which means that every extra sale incurs the same cost as previous sales. The semi-variable Expenses incurred by the extra sales are £200 for 400 sales, or £0·50 per sale. The amount of semi-variable expenses incurred by previous sales relates only to the previous sales, the extra cost of the extra business being the relevant factor.

Since the marginal cost is less than the proposed charge for the extra business, there will be a contribution to profit of (£6·00–£5·00) £1·00 per bed-night, so from the financial point of view the proposal should be accepted. The extra business will result in £400 extra profit (400 extra bed-nights × £1·00 contribution per bed-night), which is a quicker and more informative calculation than estimating the total amounts.

ANNUAL RESULTS WITH EXTRA BUSINESS

	£
Sales £160,000 + (400 × £6·00)	162,400
Food Cost £60,000 + (400 × £3·00)	61,200
Fixed Expenses £26,000 unchanged	26,000
Variable Expenses £30,000 + (400 × £1·50)	30,600
Semi-variable Expenses £28,000 + £200	28,200
	146,000
Net Profit	£16,400

Off-season Opening

In considering the advisability of staying open during the winter, many factors will be taken into account in addition to financial benefit, such as difficulty of re-engaging staff, the benefit of keeping the premises heated during the winter, and uninterrupted marketing. Whether the project is financially viable will be shown very simply by marginal costing. The extra unit of production will be the off-season period of time, and the estimated sales for the period should be compared with the marginal cost to find the contribution made.

Example

The financial results of a restaurant for last year were as follows:

	Season £	Off-season £	Total £
Sales	22,000	8,000	30,000
Variable costs	13,200	4,800	18,000
Semi-variable costs	3,000	2,000	5,000
Fixed costs	1,500	1,500	3,000
	17,700	8,300	26,000
Net Profit (Loss)	4,300	(300)	4,000

Since a loss was made in the off-season, would it have been better to close during that period?

The answer is no, because of the fixed expenses which were allocated to the off-season period, but would still have to be met out of the takings of the season if the restaurant closed. For the purpose of the example, we are assuring that costs have been analysed so as to include only inescapable costs under the heading Fixed Costs, and that Semi-variable Costs are those relating exclusively to the business done in the relevant period.

The contribution of the off-season period is shown as follows:

		£
Sales of the period		8,000
Marginal Cost		
Variable Costs	4,800	
Semi-variable	2,000	6,800
Contribution		£1,200

This illustrates the reason for the contribution being referred to as a contribution to fixed costs and profit. In this case the off-season is making a contribution of £1,200 towards the inescapable costs £1,500, leaving £300 of these costs not covered. But this is better than not covering any of the inescapable costs by closing in the off-season, in which case the total profit for the year would be £1,200 less:

ANNUAL PROFIT IF CLOSED DURING OFF-SEASON

	£
Sales (Season only)	22,000
Variable Costs	13,200
Semi-variable Costs	3,000
Fixed Costs (Whole year's Rent, Rates, etc.)	3,000
	19,200
Net Profit	2,800

EXERCISES

1. The Beach Hotel has a normal occupancy of 20,000 sleeper-nights per year, with the following trading results:

	£	Per Sleeper Night £
Takings	210,000	10·50
Cost of Food Sold	51,000	2·55
Labour Cost	54,000	2·70
Fixed Expenses	24,000	1·20
Semi-Variable Expenses	39,000	1·95
Variable Expenses	18,000	0·90
	£186,000	£9·30
Net Profit	£24,000	£1·20

A proposal is made by a tour operator to send off-season guests totalling 400 extra sleeper-nights at inclusive terms of £7·50 per day. The additional business would not interfere with normal business, but apart from food and variable expenses, there would be an increase of £540 in labour cost, and an increase of £660 in semi-variable expenses. Is the proposal financially acceptable? Prepare a statement to show what contribution would be made by the extra business.

2. The following figures relate to a seasonal restaurant:

	April–September £	October–March £
Sales	42,000	14,000
Cost of Sales	16,800	5,600
Wages and Salaries	10,000	8,000
Light and Heat	500	600
Cleaning, etc.	150	150
Other Variable Expenses	1,500	500
Fixed Expenses £4,300 p.a.		

On the basis of the above figures, would it be financially better to open for the full year, or only from April–September?

3. The Swallow Hotel has a normal occupancy of 20,000 sleeper-nights per year, and incurs the following annual costs:

	£
Cost of Food Sold	54,000
Labour Cost	51,000
Fixed Expenses	30,000
Variable Expenses	27,000
Semi-variable Expenses	57,000

Terms are £12·75 per person for Room and Breakfast and Evening Meal. The hotel does not cater for luncheon, and there are no chance meals. All meals costed to give 60% gross profit.

A firm of tour operators has made a proposal that they would send off-season guests amounting to an additional 400 sleep-nights, at special terms of £9·00 per person per day.

The additional business could be accommodated without interfering with normal business, but it is estimated that apart from food and variable expenses, there would be an increase in labour cost of £540, and semi-variable expenses would increase by £960.

(a) What are the amounts of annual takings for Rooms and for all Meals?

(b) What are the normal costs and profit per sleeper-night?

(c) Would the proposed additional business be financially acceptable? Calculate the contribution, using Marginal Costing Methods.

21. *Break-even Point*

IF all expenses varied in proportion to turnover, a business would be able to make a profit at any level of turnover. If sales fell, then expenses would fall in proportion and there would still be left a net profit, also smaller but also in proportion. Unfortunately some expenses are fixed in amount, and must be paid whether any business is done or not, while others which vary within limits, have a minimum level below which they cannot be reduced if the establishment is to remain open. Wages, for instance, may be kept very nearly proportional to turnover by judicious use of overtime and temporary staff when takings are high, but some wages to basic staff will have to be paid, however low the takings may be, so that there is a fixed minimum to what is otherwise a variable expense.

The effect of these fixed expenses is comparatively small on a high turnover, but becomes greater as turnover falls and expenses consequently account for a higher proportion of the takings; a point is eventually reached at which the turnover is just sufficient to cover all the costs without resulting in either a profit or a loss. This point is known as the *break-even point*, and is expressed as a volume of business by reference to the amount of sales or the number of customers, or the percentage occupancy achieved.

BREAK-EVEN CHART

The various levels of profit or loss to be expected from different amounts of sales can conveniently be represented on a graph, which can then be used to ascertain break-even point and the level of sales necessary to produce any required result of profit.

Example

A restaurant has fixed expenses of £2,400, and variable expenses are estimated at 15% of sales. Labour cost is 25% of sales and the rate of gross profit is 60%. Draw a graph to indicate the net profit or

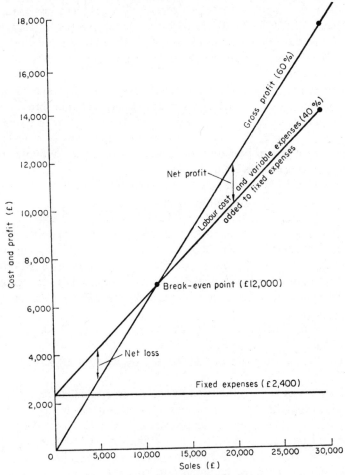

Figure 20. Break-even chart

loss achieved at various levels of turnover and mark the break-even point.

Answer

The graph is illustrated at Figure 20 and shows that the business will break even when sales amount to £12,000 for the year. When sales are less than £12,000, costs are more than gross profit, and the net loss can be ascertained by measuring the vertical distance between the two lines against the vertical scale. Thus the net loss made if sales are £5,000 is £1,400, the difference between costs (£4,400) and gross profit (£3,000). Similarly the net profit can be ascertained from the distance between the cost and profit lines for any level of sales over £12,000.

The graph gives a picture of results over a whole range of sales levels, but separate results at different levels including break-even point can be calculated arithmetically, either in total or in terms of contribution, and this is useful to do in any case as a guide to the base range necessary in preparing the graph. In the example above, the four elements of sales are food cost 40%, labour cost 25%, overheads £2,400 plus 15%, and net profit *nil* when the business breaks even. The sales at break-even point therefore amount to:

$$40\% + 25\% + 15\% + £2,400 = 80\% + £2,400$$

£2,400 therefore amounts to 20% of sales at break-even point, which must be £2,400 × 5 = £12,000.

In the same way the volume of sales which will produce a net profit of any amount can be calculated. The costs expressed as a percentage still account for 80% of sales, so fixed expenses £2,400 + net profit must be 20%.

To earn a net profit of £1,000 requires sales of £3,400 × 5 = £17,000.

To earn a net profit of £2,000 requires sales of £4,400 × 5 = £22,000.

In terms of the contribution per sale, these calculations are very much simpler, the results being given as the number of sales. If it is known that the average selling price of a meal is £3·00, the contribution will be calculated for 1 meal selling for £3·00. Otherwise the contribution can be related to the average £1·00 of sales.

In this example the marginal cost (for a £1·00 unit of sales) is 40% + 25% + 15% = 80% of £1·00 = £0·80. The contribution per £1·00 of sales is therefore £0·20, and it should be remembered that this is the contribution made by every £1 of sales to fixed costs and profit. At break-even point there is no profit, so the contributions at that level of sales must be just enough to cover the fixed costs. If we calculate how many contributions of £0·20 are required to cover fixed costs of £2,400, we shall know how many sales are needed to break even.

Break-even Point $= \dfrac{£2,400}{£0\cdot20} = 12,000$ sales of £1·00 each

$$= £12,000 \text{ Sales}$$

If the average selling price of a meal had been £3·00 in this example, the marginal cost would have been £2·40 (80% of £3·00), the contribution would have been £0·60, and the Break-even Point $\dfrac{£2,400}{£0\cdot60} =$ 4,000 meals of £3·00 each = £12,000 Sales as before.

To earn a net profit of £1,000 requires sufficient contributions to cover fixed costs £2,400 plus profit £1,000 $= \dfrac{£3,400}{£0\cdot20} =$ 17,000 sales of £1·00 each.

To earn a net profit of £2,000 requires $\dfrac{£2,400 + £2,000}{£0\cdot20} = 22,000$ sales of £1·00 each.

Note that the contribution method gives the number of sales required, and the money value of Sales will be this number multiplied by the average selling price.

MINIMUM LEVELS OF COST

The example illustrated above assumed that costs were either fixed or variable, but it may be necessary to allow for a situation where a normally variable cost, such as labour cost, becomes fixed at a minimum level when sales fall to a certain point. Below this point the labour cost cannot be reduced without closing down the business.

Example

A restaurant maintains a gross profit of 60%, and has to pay fixed expenses of £2,000. Variable expenses are 9% of sales, and labour cost is 27%, but labour cost cannot be reduced below £1,800. Prepare a break-even chart to show the profit or loss produced by sales ranging from £5,000 to £10,000.

Answer

The graph is illustrated at Figure 21, the cost line being plotted in stages. First at the vertical line representing £5,000 sales, mark off costs £3,800 (£2,000 + 36% of £5,000). Similarly mark £10,000 sales at £5,600 (£2,000 + 36% of £10,000) and draw a line connecting the two points, which represents labour cost plus overheads without allowing for the minimum. The next step is to plot a similar line

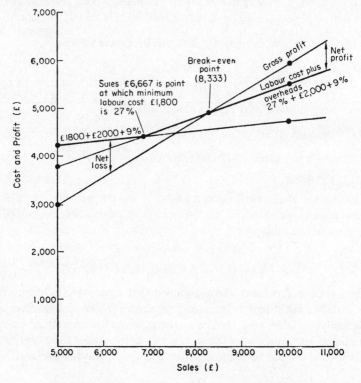

Figure 21. Break-even chart with minimum levels of cost

representing fixed labour cost £1,800 plus overheads £2,000 + 9%. This is plotted at £4,250 for £5,000 sales, and £4,700 for £10,000 sales, and a line drawn to connect the two points. This line crosses the first line at sales £6,667, which is the point at which labour cost 27% of sales is exactly £1,800. The total of labour cost plus overheads for all levels of sales is now shown by the angled line representing £2,000 + £1,800 + 9% up to £6,667, and £2,000 + 27% + 9% over £6,667. The last step is to plot gross profit by marking £3,000 on the vertical scale at £5,000 sales and £6,000 on the vertical scale at £10,000 sales, and connecting the two points.

EXERCISES

1. *(a)* Explain what is meant by break-even point.
   (b) What information can be obtained from a break-even chart?
2. *(a)* Why is it that expenses do not fall in proportion to a fall in turnover?
   (b) What is meant by semi-variable expenses?
3. Illustrate a break-even chart showing gross profit at 60% of sales, fixed expenses £1,500, and variable expenses 30% of sales. Indicate on your chart where the amount of net profit or loss may be measured.
4. Prepare a break-even chart showing gross profit at 60% of sales, fixed expenses £3,500, and variable expenses 25% of sales. Mark the break-even point and note at what level of sales this occurs.
5. Prepare a break-even chart showing gross profit at 60% of sales. Plot on your chart a net profit of £6,500 when sales are £30,000, and a net profit of £500 when sales are £10,000.
   Find:
   (a) The amount of fixed expenses.
   (b) The variable expenses when sales are £20,000.
6. A new restaurant is to be opened for which equipment is purchased costing £6,000, and additional working capital of £9,000 is provided by the proprietor.
   Rent payable will be £1,500 p.a.
   Rates will be £350 p.a.
   Insurance will be £50 p.a.
   Costings show that a supplement of 150% on food cost will give a reasonable selling price.
   Depreciation is to be provided for at 15% of the cost of equipment.
   Variable expenses are to be estimated at 40% of sales.
   Prepare a break-even chart and plot lines to represent gross profit and total expenses.
   Find:
   (a) The break-even point.
   (b) The turnover necessary to realize a net profit equivalent to 15% of capital employed.

22. Canteens and Subsidies

IF a canteen is self-supporting, then its cost problems are those of any restaurant, even though they may be somewhat eased by having a captive clientele. But many industrial canteens are not expected to be self-supporting, the charges made being uneconomic deliberately as a benefit to the workers using the canteen, and the Company subsidizing the canteen loss. This policy may be directly contrasted with the growing practice of giving workers luncheon vouchers, and the method adopted may well depend on comparative costs if both alternatives are available. The cost of giving luncheon vouchers is simple to calculate, the cost per day being a straight multiplication of the value of voucher given to each employee by the number of employees. If different groups of employees are to have different voucher values, then each voucher value will be multiplied by the number of employees in the group.

From the employer's point of view this system has all the merits of simplicity and certainty of cost, and if independent restaurants are available to accommodate all the employees, there may be no incentive to consider any alternative. But it is frequently the case that an internal canteen is needed because there are no adequate alternatives, or it may be thought better or more convenient to provide meals on the premises. In this case the question of cost will very soon arise, allied to the question of how much to charge the employees.

At first sight, a deliberate policy of providing meals at uneconomic prices appears to make nonsense of costing, but it should be remembered that the degree of unprofitability should be known and controlled. As a matter of policy it will be decided what range of prices the canteen users should be charged, and again as a matter of policy it will be decided how much the firm is prepared to contribute as a subsidy. These two factors must be reconciled somehow and a canteen pricing policy formulated which will satisfy both conditions.

If the canteen is not to make a profit, it may be required to break even or to make a net loss not exceeding a certain amount per year.

In these circumstances there will be no question of calculating selling prices on the basis of a gross profit of about 60%, but the *method* holds good even if the proportions change. It is still a question of considering the elements of sales and remembering that sales must cover all costs plus net profit. In the case of a canteen which is to break even the net profit will be nil. If it is to make a calculated loss, then the net profit is a minus figure, so that sales must be equal to total cost less the amount of loss to be subsidized by the employer. In this connection it should be emphasized that a subsidy from the employer does not constitute additional sales for the canteen, but is a reduction of the costs which the canteen must pay for. In any estimates or other calculations for a canteen, a subsidy should be deducted from costs, or treated as net loss being paid for by the employer.

At this point canteen costing follows the familiar pattern of relating certain known costs to other estimated costs, and thus ascertaining ratios which can be applied to all units of sales.

ESTIMATING FUTURE RESULTS

All estimates for a canteen are greatly assisted by the uniformity of turnover to be expected, and the actual costs of a week or month provide a quick check on the validity of the estimates for the year. Food cost will usually be a starting point and an estimate for the year will need to be built up from the estimated average cost per meal served. As a first estimate, this may start as the result of considering the type of meals to be served and what food cost would be expected for each meal. The average food cost per meal can then be multiplied by the number of meals expected to be sold in a year. Where there is a normal variety of meals offered, the proportions in which different dishes will sell (sales mix) will need to be allowed for in estimating average food cost, and checking of actual experience is very important.

Labour cost cannot be estimated as a percentage of sales in the case of a new canteen and will need to be built up from estimates of canteen staff required and rates of pay applicable to each.

Overheads will be estimated in the same way as for preparing a profit budget, except that certain expenses may not have to be allowed for because they are provided by the Company. Premises are often provided in this way without charge, as are services of office staff for keeping canteen records.

If the canteen is to break even, then food cost, labour cost, and overheads constitute the elements of sales, since net profit is to be *nil*. The total of the estimates of these costs is therefore the total amount to be recovered from sales, and if divided by the number of meals expected to be sold, will show the expected average selling price per meal. When this is compared with the expected average food cost per meal, the supplement percentage to be added to food cost to price each meal will be discovered. This pricing policy of adding a given percentage can be applied to the food cost of each dish, which will give a selling price for each dish so that the average selling price is in proportion to the average food cost.

Example

An industrial canteen caters for an average of 100 lunches per day for five days per week, fifty weeks per year. It is estimated that food cost will average 10p per meal; labour cost will amount to £20 per week; gas and electricity will be £130 per annum; repairs and renewals £120 per annum; laundry and cleaning £60; depreciation £150; sundry expenses £100. No other expenses will be payable by the canteen.

Calculate the average selling price which will have to be charged to enable the canteen to break even, and recommend a pricing policy to achieve this result.

Answer

No. of meals	= 100 × 5 × 50	= 25,000 meals	
Food cost	= 25,000 × £0·10		= £2,500
Labour cost	= £20 × 50		= 1,000
Overheads			
Gas and electricity		130	
Repairs and renewals		120	
Laundry and cleaning		60	
Depreciation		150	
Sundry expenses		100	
		—	560
Total sales will need to be			£4,060

Average selling price   £4,060 ÷ 25,000   =   £0·16
Average food cost   0·10
                                                        ———
Supplement   0·06

Supplement as a percentage of food cost $= \dfrac{0.06 \times 100}{0.10} = 60\%$

Pricing policy: add to food cost of each dish a *supplement of* 60%.

EXERCISES

1. The Blagdon Engineering Co. Ltd has 300 employees who work 5 days per week for 50 weeks per year.

   The Company operates a works canteen for lunches only which will accommodate 200 employees, who pay 15p per day for lunch, the Company subsidizing canteen losses. The other employees are given a 10p luncheon voucher towards the cost of buying meals out. The annual cost of food is £4,500, canteen wages £2,850, overheads £2,250.

   The Company is considering enlarging the scope of the canteen to accommodate all the employees. Additional labour costing £950 would be needed, general overheads would increase by £200, and additional capital expenditure would be needed amounting to £1,800. It will be necessary to take into account interest on the additional capital expenditure at 6% and depreciation at 10%. As canteen manager you are asked to calculate:

   (a) The present cost per day that the Company incurs for each employee eating in the canteen, to compare with the 10p luncheon voucher given to other employees.

   (b) The present annual cost to the Company of employees' lunches.

   (c) The annual cost to the Company if all employees have lunch in the canteen.

   (d) The daily cost per employee.

2. Vitamins Ltd operate a works canteen for the provision of meals to their employees. They serve an average of 500 meals per day, 5 days per week for 50 weeks of the year, several choices being offered each day.

   The annual cost of food is £9,375, wages £6,250, overheads £7,812.

The company wish to provide meals at an average charge of 12p each, and are willing to subsidize the canteen to the extent of £5,000 p.a.

The company occupying an adjoining factory have approached Vitamins Ltd and asked if they would be prepared to serve their employees with meals (400 per day) of the same quality at 12p each. They are prepared to take the meals at a different time to the Vitamins employees, so there would be no difficulty regarding accommodation. Additional labour costing £2,500 p.a. would be required in the canteen.

As canteen manager, you are asked to suggest a pricing policy (i.e. the percentages to be added to the cost of each dish) and give your recommendation as to whether the company should be prepared to supply the meals to the neighbouring firm on the terms suggested. You should supply detailed figures to support your recommendations.

(H.C.I.M.A.)

3. The Britannia Cycle Co. Ltd are about to establish a canteen for their workers. The aim initially is to provide a midday meal, 5 days per week for 50 weeks each year, with a choice of several dishes each day, charges being on an *à la carte* basis. There are 330 workers and it is estimated that 90% of them will use the canteen. It is proposed to start with the following staff:

1 Manager	@	£20 per week
4 Kitchen staff	@	£8 per week each
3 Counter staff	@	£7 per week each
1 Storeman	@	£9 per week

£5,000 of equipment has been purchased, and the cost of this will be written off over a suitable period. It is also anticipated that £50 per year will be required to cover the cost of replacing crockery, etc. Consumption of gas for cooking has been estimated at £800 p.a.

The Directors of the Company do not intend to make any charge for the use of the premises, nor for electricity and water. They do not wish to make a profit out of the canteen, but they would like it to be self-supporting. The main intention is to provide good meals at a low price.

Bearing in mind the above points, you are required to:

(a) Suggest a pricing scheme for the meals.
(b) Prepare a budget for the first year of operation.
(c) Outline a system of routine check on the financial results during the year.

(H.C.I.M.A.)

23. *Standard Costing*

STANDARD Costing is a system of estimating standard amounts for all costs, and preparing costing statements from the standard costs instead of actual costs. Control is exercised by analysing the differences between these figures and the actual results. The differences are analysed into *variances* from the expected profit, identifying each variance as *favourable* or *adverse*, depending on whether the actual result is more profit or less profit than expected. The process is referred to as *variance analysis*, and can be very useful in identifying and allocating responsibility for differences in profit.

The variances will be concerned with differences in Sales, Ingredient Cost, Labour Cost, or Overheads. The examples given here will relate to food, but the same principles apply to labour cost and overheads with some slight changes in the terms used. For food we would refer to Ingredient Price Variance, but to Wage Rate Variance instead of Wage Price Variance. Similarly the term Efficiency is used as an alternative to Usage.

Any change in Sales will be due to (1) a change in the selling price of each meal, or (2) a change in the number of meals sold. The first is called a Sales Price Variance, and will allow for the change in average selling price for all the meals actually sold at the different price. The second is called a Sales Volume Variance, and will automatically create an additional cost of food for the extra meals, so the variance will take into account the different number of meals and the gross profit expected from every meal.

A change in the total cost of ingredients used may be due to any of three causes:

(1) A change in the number of units sold.
(2) A change in the buying price of the food.
(3) A change in the quantity of food used in every meal.

The first is part of the sales volume variance which has already been dealt with, the second is an Ingredient Price Variance, and the third an Ingredient Usage Variance. These variances are Favourable or Adverse according to their effect on profit.

If the actual selling price is different from the standard, but no other changes have taken place, the gross profit will be different by the amount of the Sales Price Variance, which is the difference in selling price for all the meals actually sold.

Example 1

	Standard		*Actual*	
Sales	1,000 meals		1,000 meals	
	@ £2·00	£2,000	@ £1·90 =	£1,900
Food Cost	250 kg @		250 kg @	
	£3·00 per kg	750	£3·00 per kg	750
Gross Profit		£1,250		£1,150

Sales Price Variance = Difference in Price per Meal × Actual No. of Meals
= £0·10 less (Adverse Variance) × 1,000 meals
= £100 (Adv)

If 100 more meals are sold than expected, the difference in Sales will be 100 × Selling Price per meal, but the profit will not increase by this amount because more meals will mean more food cost. The variance in the profit will be 100 × Standard Gross Profit per meal, which allows for the extra food used to produce the extra meals, assuming that the standard quantity of food is used in each meal. Any further difference in the cost of food actually used will be due to a change in the price paid for food or a change in the quantity used in each meal.

Example 2

	Standard		*Actual*	
Sales	1,000 meals		1,200 meals	
	@ £2·00 =	£2,000	@ £2·00 =	£2,400
Food Cost	250 kg @		300 kg @	
	£3·00 per kg	750	£3·00 per kg	900
Gross Profit (£1.25 per meal)		£1,250	(£1.25 per meal)	£1,500

It will be seen that the quantity of food used per meal is 250 g in both standard and actual figures, and the price per kg is the same in both cases. The total cost of food used has increased because of the increased number of meals, but the cost per meal remains the same. The only variation in gross profit is due to the volume of sales:

Sales Volume Variance = Difference in No. of Meals × Standard Gross Profit per meal
= 200 more meals (Favourable Variance) × £1·25
= £250 (Fav)

Similarly with changes in the cost of food, the variation in gross profit may be due to a change in ingredient price per kg or to a change in the quantity used per meal.

Example 3

	Standard		Actual	
Sales	1,000 meals		1,000 Meals	
	@ £2·00 =	£2,000	@ £2·00 =	£2,000
Food Cost	250 kg @		300 kg @	
	£3·00 per kg	750	£3·10 per kg	930
Gross Profit		£1,250		£1,070

The gross profit is less because of an increase in food cost, which in turn can be analysed as due to paying more per kg for the food and also using more food in each meal:

Ingredient Price Variance = Difference in Price × Actual Usage
= £0·10 more (Adv) × 300 kg =
30(Adv)
Ingredient Usage Variance = Difference in Quantity used per meal × Actual No. of Meals × Standard Price per kg
= 50 g more per meal (Adv) × 1,000 meals × £3·00 per kg =
150(Adv)

Total reduction in gross profit   £180

In any given set of circumstances it is possible for all these factors to change, so that the net change in profit comprises all four variances.

Example 4

	Standard		*Actual*	
Sales	1,000 meals		1,100 meals	
	@ £2·00 =	£2,000	@ £1·90 =	£2,090
Food Cost	250 kg @		330 kg @	
	£3·00 per kg	750	£3·10 per kg	1·023
		——		——
Gross Profit		£1,250		£1,067

In this example the extra usage of ingredients 80 kg is partly due to increased volume of sales, and partly due to increased usage on each meal:

Extra ingredients allowed for in Sales Volume Variance
$$100 \text{ meals} \times 250 \text{ g} = 25 \text{ kg}$$
Extra ingredients allowed for in Ingredient Usage Variance
$$1{,}100 \text{ meals} \times 50 \text{ g} = 55 \text{ kg}$$

$$80 \text{ kg}$$

Sales Volume Variance	100 × £1·25	125 (Fav)
Sales Price Variance	£0·10 × 1100	(110)(Adv)
Ingredient Usage Variance	50 g × 1100 meals × £3·00 per kg	(165)(Adv)
Ingredient Price Variance	£0·10 × (30 g × 1100 meals = 330 kg)	(33)(Adv)
Net reduction in profit		£183

The standard food cost is the standard quantity multiplied by the standard purchase price = £750, but in calculating the usage variance the standard usage is the standard quantity per meal for the number of meals actually sold. So the usage variance is the difference between actual and standard usage per meal for the number of meals actually sold, at the standard price per kg. An alternative way of finding the standard usage is by taking proportions of total quantities:

Total quantity for standard 1,000 meals as above   250 kg

Standard quantity for 1,100 meals $\frac{1,100}{1,000} \times 250$ kg   275 kg

Actual quantity for 1,100 meals   330 kg

Usage Variance 330 kg – 275 kg = 55 kg @ standard price
£3·00 per kg   £165 (Adv)

EXERCISES

1. The standard cost figures of a snack bar for April were as follows:

No. of dishes sold	9,000
Selling Price per dish	55p
Cost of ingredients per kg	40p
Quantity of ingredients used	2,250 kg

Actual results for the same period were:

No of dishes sold	9,800
Selling Price per dish	60p
Cost of ingredients per kg	50p
Quantity of ingredients used	2,450 kg

List the variances accounting for the difference in gross profit.

2. From the following information, prepare a statement showing the variances which account for the differences between budgeted and actual gross profit.

Budget		*Actual*	
1,000 meals @ £2·00 = £2,000		1,200 meals @ £2·05 = £2,460	
Cost 200 kg @ £3·60	720	Cost 180 kg @ £4·80	864
Gross Profit	£1,280		£1,596

3. Prepare a variance analysis statement from the following information:

	Standard	*Actual*
No. of Meals Sold	1,000	2,000
Selling Price per meal	£2·20	£2·20
Ingredients used	250 kg	600 kg
Ingredients cost per kg	£3·60	£4·05

4. The following is a reconciliation of the budgeted and actual gross
   profit for the Cozy Café:

			£
Budget Gross Profit – 3,000 covers @ £0·89			2,670
Add Spending Power Variance			
Actual	£1·60		
Budget	£1·50		
4,000 covers @	£0·10		400
Add Cover Volume Variance			
Actual	4,000 covers		
Budget	3,000 covers		
	1,000 covers @ £0·89		890
			3,960
Less Ingredient Price Variance			
Actual	£3·16 per kg		
Budget	£3·05 per kg		
1,000 kg @	£0·11 per kg		110
			3,850
Less Ingredient Usage Variance			
Actual Usage at actual volume 1,000 kg			
Budget Usage at actual volume 800 kg			
	200 kg @ £3·05		610
Actual Gross Profit – 4,000 covers @ £0·81			£3,240

You are required to prepare (a) the budgeted trading account and
(b) the actual trading account.

5. A restaurant prepares a budget from which standards are established. For May 19.. the budgeted standards set, and the actual
   results achieved are as follows:

	Budgeted £		Actual £
Sales:			
750 dishes @ £0·53	397·50	780 dishes @ £0·53	413·40
Less cost of sales	198·75		197·60
	£198·75		£215·80

The standard cost per dish (only two ingredients are used) were calculated as follows:

	Standard cost per dish
Ingredient A 200 g @ £0·62½ per kg	£0·125
Ingredient B 100 g @ £1·40 per kg	£0·140

The actual costs were as follows:

	Actual price	Actual Food Used
Ingredient A	£0·65 per kg	160 kg
Ingredient B	£1·30 per kg	72 kg

You are required to:

(*a*) Calculate the following variances:
    (i) Sales volume variance
    (ii) ingredient price variances
    (iii) ingredient usage variances
(*b*) reconcile the budgeted profit with the actual profit
(*c*) comment briefly on the significance of the variances

(H.C.I.M.A.)

24. *Summaries for Revision*

Chapter 1

Costing is systematically finding out the costs relating to a suitable unit of sales.

Costing is necessary in order to have constant, up-to-date information on profitability.

Units of sales are measurable parts of total sales, such as a dish, a banquet, or sales for a month, to which costs can conveniently be related.

Chapter 2

Elements of sales are food cost and gross profit. Gross profit comprises labour cost, overheads, and net profit.

Total cost means all costs, comprising food cost, labour cost, and overheads.

Food cost is the cost of ingredients used in producing the food sold, without any addition for preparation or cooking costs.

Labour cost is the cost of employing staff, including wages, salaries, National Insurance, Selective Employment Tax, cost of staff meals, cost of staff accommodation.

Overheads are expenses other than food cost and labour cost, such as rent, rates, insurance, repairs, gas and electricity, etc.

Gross profit is the amount left out of sales when only food cost has been deducted.

Net profit is the amount left out of gross profit when all costs have been deducted.

High margin return means a higher gross profit percentage than is normal.

Representative customer's contribution to sales is the charge for the average meal, or total sales divided by the total number of customers.

Reward for capital invested is a notional interest on capital which a business should provide for its proprietor apart from net profit.

Proprietor's remuneration is that part of the proprietor's return from a business which relates to his working in the business, as distinct from the net profit due to him as owner.

Kitchen percentages are the costs of the different kinds of food consumed, expressed as a percentage of total food cost or as a percentage of sales. Comparison of these percentages for consecutive periods is part of food cost control.

Chapter 3

Rate of gross profit is the gross profit expressed as a percentage of sales. It is important to establish this in order to know what part of the selling price of a small unit of sales, such as one portion of a dish, must be allowed for in order to cover labour cost, overheads, and net profit.

Dish costing calculations

$$\text{Gross profit percentage} = \frac{\text{gross profit} \times 100\%}{\text{selling price}}$$

$$\text{Selling price} = \frac{\text{food cost} \times 100}{\text{food cost percentage}}$$

Pricing policy is the policy of the management in fixing the selling price of meals.

Supplement is the amount added to food cost, sometimes used in order to find the selling price, and expressed as a percentage of food cost.

Chapter 4

Banquets calculations
(a) Deduct items estimated as percentage of sales from 100% to find remaining items as a percentage of sales.

$$(b)\ \text{Selling price} = \frac{\text{amount of remaining items} \times 100}{\text{remaining items as a percentage}}$$

Chapter 5

Bone loss is the reduction in the weight of meat due to the removal of bone.

Cooking loss is the reduction in the weight of meat due to cooking.
Calculations
Cooked meat price per kg

$$= \frac{\text{raw meat price per kg} \times \text{raw meat weight}}{\text{cooked meat weight}}$$

or Cooked meat price per kg

$$= \frac{\text{raw meat price per kg} \times 100}{\text{cooked meat percentage of raw meat}}$$

Wholesale price per kg

$$= \frac{\text{total wholesale cost} \times \text{retail price per kg}}{\text{total retail cost}}$$

Chapter 6

Portion control means ensuring that portions served are consistently the same size.

Method of portion control is to use suitable equipment and maintain effective supervision.

Portion control equipment
> Scales
> Slicing machines
> Measuring jugs
> Graded scoops and ladles
> Standard-size baking tins
> Standard-size cups, glasses, soup bowls
> Standard recipe charts
> Bar optics

Chapter 7

Order book is a book of forms on which orders of goods from suppliers can be written, torn out of the book, and sent to suppliers.

Goods received book is used for entering record of goods from delivery note.

Goods purchased are detailed on a *delivery note* from the supplier for checking purposes.

Bin card is used for recording receipts, issues, and stock remaining of non-perishable goods.

Stores requisition is a form used by a department of a business ordering goods from the main store of the business.

Stock sheets are lists of all trading stocks on hand at the date of stocktaking, valued at cost.

LIFO stands for Last In, First Out, referring to which price to use for issues or stocks when prices have changed.

FIFO stands for First In, First Out, an alternative to LIFO.

Chapter 8

Cost of food consumed = opening stock *plus* purchases *less* closing stock.

Cost of food sold = cost of food consumed *less* staff meals.

Gross profit percentage $\dfrac{\text{gross profit}}{\text{sales}} \times 100\%$

Staff meals must be adjusted for in costing figures if gross profit is to be correctly calculated.

Adjustment for staff meals – deduct the cost of staff meals from food cost and add it to labour cost.

Chapter 9

Bar control at selling price means reconciling the value of bar stocks sold, calculated at selling price, with the actual sales made.

Bar costs separate from food costs enables the gross profit obtained on each to be calculated. This is important because the bar percentage will be less than the food percentage.

Bar gross profit less than food gross profit because the expenses to be paid out of it are less (no cooking costs).

Chapter 10

Inclusive cost of labour means the total cost of employing staff, whether paid in cash, free meals, or accommodation.

Wages percentage of sales at different times in the year may be different from the percentage for the year, but should be comparable with other similar periods.

Direct labour cost means labour cost directly related to one source of income without the need for apportionment.

Indirect labour cost means labour cost which relates to more than one source of income and so needs to be apportioned. It should be treated in the same way as overheads.

Chapter 11

Overheads are expenses other than food cost and labour cost.

Fixed expenses are those which are fixed in amount whatever the volume of business done, such as rent, rates, insurance, depreciation. They do not vary with sales.

Variable expenses are those which vary according to the volume of sales.

Semi-variable expenses are expenses which vary within limits, but cannot be reduced below a certain point however little business is done.

Fixed expenses apportioned on a time basis, that is the expense for four weeks is one-thirteenth of the expense for a year.

Chapter 12

Inclusive charges must be apportioned between food takings and apartments takings if the relationship of costs to income is to be controlled.

Sales mix is the ratio of different ·kinds of sales in a mixed total.

Sleeper nights are convenient units to which costs can be related, being number of guests multiplied by the length of stay of each guest.

Occupancy rate is the number of sleeper nights of a period expressed as a percentage of the maximum possible in that period.

Chapter 13

Costs should be allocated to the appropriate source of income in order to see that the costs are reasonable and to determine what net profit has been made on each activity.

Indirect costs are those which relate to the hotel as a whole, and not directly to rooms, or directly to restaurant.

Apportionment may be made on the basis of the floor area of the revenue-earning departments.

Chapter 14

Own accommodation is the cost of the proprietor's own accommodation included in the expenses of the hotel. It should be deducted from the total cost in calculating net profit.

Revision of charges must be based on the fact that the average charge multiplied by the total number of guests must equal total cost plus net profit.

Chapter 15

Budgets may be revenue budgets or capital budgets. Revenue budgets are forecasts of future profits; capital budgets are forecasts of future assets.

Budgetary control is the comparison of cost figures with budgets and the investigation of variances.

Accounting periods of four weeks or five weeks are more satisfactory than calendar months for comparison purposes.

Chapter 16

Cash budgets are forecasts of the cash balance at future dates, calculated from estimates of cash to be received and cash to be paid.

Differences from profit budgets arise from the difference in purpose. Receipts and payments in the month must be allowed for, whether revenue or capital, and income or expenditure of the month which are not actually received or paid in the month must be excluded.

Chapter 17

Daily cash budget is a cash budget in more detail so that short-term planning of cash utilization is possible.

Advantages

  (a) Payments can be planned for the most convenient time.
  (b) The need for overdraft arrangements can be foreseen.
  (c) Unwanted cash balances can be safely invested on a short-term basis.

Chapter 18

Cash flow statement is a forecast of the cash to be received and paid during a coming year.

When prepared from profit budget must allow for non-cash expenses (e.g. depreciation) included in the profit budget, and capital items involving cash not included in the profit budget.

Reduction in creditors means that more cash has been paid than is allowed for in the calculation of profit and this will reduce the cash balance.

Increase in creditors means that less cash has been paid than the costs shown in the profit budget, and this will increase the cash balance.

Chapter 19

Operating statement is a statement of costs and profit with budget figures for comparison purposes.

Cost comparisons draw attention to costs that are too great or too small and need management action.

Profit comparisons show the trend and help to assess the accuracy of the forecast profit for the year.

Chapter 20

Marginal cost is the increase or reduction in total cost, at a given volume of output, resulting from an increase or reduction of one unit of output.

The contribution to Fixed Costs and Profit per unit of sales is the selling price of the unit less the marginal cost.

Chapter 21

Break-even point is that volume of sales at which total cost is equal to total sales and no profit or loss is made.

Break-even chart is a graph illustrating the amount of profit or loss to be expected for varying volumes of sales; it is prepared by plotting gross profit and costs for each level of sales.

Minimum level of costs is the amount of cost which cannot be reduced if the business is to continue functioning.

Chapter 22

Subsidy is a contribution by the employer towards the costs of a canteen. It will result in charges to employees being less since they will have fewer costs to cover.

Subsidy is not income of the canteen, but a reduction of costs. This is important in budgeting, since the subsidy is not related to individual meals, and costing must be related to the selling price of meals.

Chapter 23

Sales Price Variance is the difference to profit caused by a change in the selling price of each meal:
Difference in Price × Actual No. of meals.

Sales Volume Variance is the difference to profit caused by a change in the No. of meals sold:
Difference in No. of meals × Standard Gross Profit per meal.

Ingredient Price Variance is the difference to profit caused by a change in the price per kg paid for purchases of food.
Difference in Price × Actual Usage

Ingredient Usage Variance is the difference to profit caused by a change in the quantity of ingredients used in each meal.
Difference in Quantity used in each meal × No. of meals actually sold × Standard Price per kg.

Solutions to Exercises

Chapter 2

6. Net profit £525
7. Gross profit £34,500; 57·5%
8. (a) 63·2%   (b) 59·0%   (c) 63·0%
13. (a) £1·80   (b) £0·192
14.

	April 4	April 11	April 18
	%	%	%
Meat	20·8	23·0	19·0
Fish and poultry	25·0	24·5	26·2
Fruit and vegetables	15·0	13·7	15·2
Groceries	17·1	17·2	15·5
Dairy	10·0	9·8	13·1
Bakery	7·0	6·8	6·5
Tea and coffee	5·1	5·0	4·5
	100·0%	100·0%	100·0%

Chapter 3

1. (a) £9·321   (b) £0·777   (c) 61·2%
2. (a) £0·443   (b) £1·166
3. (a) £0·993   (b) 54·9%   (c) £0·283
4. (a) £0·110   (b) £0·264
5. (a) £0·060   (b) £0·150   (c) £0·163
6. (b) £0·363   B £0·286   C £0·215
8. £0·120
9. £0·226
10. £0·072
11. (a) £0·345   (b) £0·863
12. £0·171 per portion
13. (a) 54·4%   (b) increase to £0·593 per portion
14. (a) £0·453   (b) £1·200
15. (a) £0·981 per portion   (b) £1·019 per portion

Chapter 4

1. (*a*) £4·80   (*b*) 50%
2. (*a*) £5·25   (*b*) 59·5%   (*c*) wages 25·3%; overheads 19·1%
3. £4·95
4. (*a*) £4·281   (*b*) £74·925
5. (*a*) £3·741   (*b*) £0·415   (*c*) £4·156   (*d*) £2·637   (*e*) £1·519
6. (*a*) £4·50   (*b*) £22·50   (*c*) 37·9%
7. £5·00
8. (*a*) £4·50   (*b*) £594·00

Chapter 5

1. (*b*) £3·345
2. £2·857
3. (*a*) £0·292   (*b*) £3·240
4. (*a*) £0·269   (*b*) £2·991
5. Cost of usable meat £2·033 per kg; cost of cooked meat £3·388 per kg
6. £2·540
7. Steak meat £2·890 per kg; stewing meat £1·135 per kg
8. Steak meat £2·861 per kg; stewing meat £1·158 per kg
9. Steak meat £2·908 per kg; stewing meat £1·163 per kg
10. Cost of 200 g steak £0·584

Chapter 8

1. £16,386
2. £1,481
3. £1,801
4. (*a*) £84·00
5. Cost of food sold £1,560
6. Cost of food sold £1,724
7. (*a*) Cost of food sold £1,094   (*b*) gross profit £1,666   (*c*) gross profit percentage 60·4%
8. Gross profit £1,482; gross profit percentage 65·0%

10. (*b*)

	Total £	Meat £	Vegetables £	Sweets £	Other Foods £
Sales	3,119·90	968·70	1,200·00	303·70	647·50
Stock 1st April	734·10	215·30	188·90	46·70	283·20
Net purchases	1,018·30	355·60	443·20	85·10	134·40
	1,752·40	570·90	632·10	131·80	417·60
Stock 30 April	607·90	163·40	212·10	30·60	201·80
Cost of Food sold	1,144·50	407·50	420·00	101·20	215·80
Gross profit	1,975·40	561·20	780·00	202·50	431·70
Gross profit percentage	63·3%	57·9%	65%	66·7%	66·7%

12. (*a*) Cost of food consumed £1,944; actual gross profit (£1,656) 46%; less than expected gross profit by £216

Chapter 9

4. (*a*) 50·6%   (*b*) £910   (*c*) 1·2%
5. 9% on calculated sales
7. Whisky £33·60; gin £38·40; sherry £13·00; wine £25·20; table wine £61·92; total £172·12

Chapter 10

3. £1,644
4. 26%

Chapter 11

1. Food cost £760; gross profit £1,340; net profit £330; net profit percentage 15·7%
2. (*a*) Gross profit £1,000   (*b*) net profit £190   (*c*) net profit percentage 10%

3. Gross profit £1,245 (62%); net profit £300 (15%)
4. Food cost £1,083 (38%); gross profit £1,767 (62%); labour cost £746 (26%); overheads £679 (24%); net profit £342 (12%)
5. (*a*) Gross profit £1,320 (60%)
   (*b*) Food cost £880 (40%); labour cost £550 (25%); overheads £440 (20%)
   (*c*) Net profit £330 (15%)
6. (*a*) Gross profit £2,640 (60%)
   (*b*) Food cost £1,760 (40%); labour cost £1,100 (25%); overheads £880 (20%)
   (*c*) Net profit £660 (15%)
   Net profit per representative customer £0·25
7. (*a*) Food cost (£642) 35·7%   (*b*) labour cost (£453) 25·1%
   (*c*) overhead cost (£328) 18·2%   (*d*) total cost (£1,423) 79%
   (*e*) net profit (£377) 21%

Chapter 12

1. (*a*) Meals £40·60 per week; accommodation £23·40 per week
   (*b*) £4·14
2. £90·00 per week
3. (*a*) £1,559·60   (*b*) £2·80
4. 70%
5. £3·932

Chapter 13

3. Accommodation £6,150; meals £1,575; bar £750
4. £0·50
5. (*a*) £3·00   (*b*) £3·529
6. £22·00 per week (average 38·5 guests per week to pay total charges £44,044 p.a.)
7. Costs per week:

	Total £	Meals £	Accom. £
Cost of meals 60% of 490 × £2·80	823·20	823·20	—
Direct wages	538·20	343·00	195·20
Indirect wages £176 in ratio 1,200:3,600(=1:3)	176·00	44·00	132·00
Direct expenses	188·00	100·00	88·00

[contd. overleaf]

Indirect expenses $\frac{1}{52}$ (£34,112)

= £656 in ratio 1,200:3,600	656·00	164·00	492·00
	2,381·40	1,474·20	907·20
Net profit 10% on sales (one-ninth of total cost)	264·60	163·80	100·80
Total weekly takings required	2,646·00	1,638·00	1,008·00

No. of guests per week 60% of
$\frac{1}{7}$ (490) = 42

Inclusive terms per person	£63·00	£39·00	£24·00

Chapter 14

1. (*a*) 30%   (*b*) £17·40
2. £2,760
3. (*a*) £2,200   (*b*) £750   (*c*) 34·1%
5. (*a*) £1,400   (*b*) £61·00 per week

Chapter 15

2. (*a*) £1,200
   (*b*) Food cost £600; gross profit £900; rent £100; wages £540; replacements £20; depreciation £30; fuel £60; net profit £150

3. PROFIT BUDGET FOR YEAR ENDING 31 DECEMBER 19—

	March £	*June* £	*Sept.* £	*Dec.* £	*Year* £
Sales	3,825	7,650	10,200	3,825	25,500
Gross profit (60%)	2,295	4,590	6,120	2,295	15,300
Labour cost	765	1,530	2,040	765	5,100
Fixed expenses	750	750	750	750	3,000
Variable expenses	575	1,145	1,530	575	3,825
	2,090	3,425	4,320	2,090	11,925
Net profit	205	1,165	1,800	205	3,375
Net profit %	5·4%	15·2%	17·6%	5·4%	13·2%

4. *Year:* sales £122,304; gross profit £73,382; labour £30,576; fixed expenses £12,000; variable expenses £18,346; net profit £12,460
   4 weeks: sales £5,376; gross profit £3,226; labour £1,344; fixed expenses £923; variable expenses £806; net profit £153

Chapter 16

2. July increase £1,700; August increase £3,500; September reduction £300

3. July £663; August £1,209; September £1,716; October £1,287

4.

CASH BUDGET

	June £	July £	Aug. £	Sept. £
Receipts				
Sales	31,465	29,658	42,147	58,393
Investment income		1,000		
	31,465	30,658	42,147	58,393
Payments				
Purchases	49,251	52,375	19,142	11,641
Rent	1,200			1,200
Expenses	10,213	10,869	11,019	10,542
Dividend		2,500		
	60,664	65,744	30,161	23,383
Surplus/Deficit	(D) 29,199	(D) 35,086	11,986	35,010
Balance B/Fwd.	51,269	22,070	13,016*	1,030*
Balance C/Fwd.	£22,070	£13,016*	£1,030*	£33,980

* Overdrawn

Chapter 16 (contd.)

5.

	CASH BUDGET		
	July	*Aug.*	*Sept.*
	£	£	£
Receipts			
Sales	18,405	19,811	15,402
Investment income	2,000		
	20,405	19,811	15,402
Payments			
Purchases	5,086	5,023	4,982
Expenses	3,842	4,185	3,976
Rent	900		
Rates	600		
Wages	4,061	5,004	3,896
Dividend	3,000		
	17,489	14,212	12,854
Surplus	2,916	5,599	2,548
Balance B/Fwd.	23,609	26,525	32,124
	£26,525	£32,124	£34,672

Chapter 17

2.

DAILY CASH BUDGET

			Receipts £	Payments £	Balance £
April	1	Balance			874
	7	Takings	600		
		Wages		200	
		Expenses		30	1,244
	14	Takings	600		
		Wages		200	
		Expenses		30	
		March creditors		1,440	174
	21	Takings	600		
		Wages		200	
		Expenses		30	544
	28	Takings	1,500		
		Wages		250	
		Expenses		30	1,764

4. 21 July

DAILY CASH BUDGET

			Receipts £	Payments £	Balance £
July	1	Balance			1,500
	7	Takings	800		
		Wages		200	2,100
	10	Creditors		1,800	300
	14	Takings	800		
		Wages		200	900
	21	Takings	800		
		Wages		200	
		Deposit account		1,000	500
	28	Takings	800		
		Wages		200	
		Salaries		180	920

Chapter 18

3. Forecast cash balance at end of year £8,112

Chapter 19

3.   OPERATING STATEMENT FOR 4 WEEKS ENDING 28 JUNE

	Actual		*Budget*	
	%	£	%	£
Sales	100	3,078	100	2,700
Gross profit	61	1,871	60	1,620
Wages, salaries, and staff meals	30	921	25	675
Overheads	25	770	25	675
	55	1,691	50	1,350
Net profit	6	£180	10	£270

4.   OPERATING STATEMENT FOR APRIL

	Actual		*Budget*	
	%	£	%	£
Takings				
Apartments	37	6,147	38	6,000
Food	58	9,681	56	9,000
Wines	5	872	6	1,000
Total	100	16,700	100	16,000
Gross Profit				
Apartments	100	6,147	100	6,000
Food	59	5,755	60	5,400
Wines	50	440	50	500
	74	12,342	74	11,900
Labour cost	19	3,173	20	3,200
Overheads	40	6,714	43	6,900
	59	9,887	63	10,100
Net profit	15	£2,455	11	£1,800

Forecast profit for year underestimated

5.

OPERATING STATEMENT FOR APRIL

| | \multicolumn{4}{Actual} | | | \multicolumn{4}{Budget} | | |
| | Aparts. | | Food | | Aparts. | | Food | |
	%	£	%	£	%	£	%	£
Takings	100	1,620	100	2,430	100	1,500	100	2,300
Cost of food			47	1,142			45	1,035
Gross profit	100	1,620	53	1,288	100	1,500	55	1,265
Wages	31	500	25	600	30	450	25	575
Fixed expenses	•9	150	10	230	10	150	10	230
Variable expenses	45	730	5	125	45	675	5	115
	85	1,380	40	955	85	1,275	40	920
Net profit	15	240	13	333	15	225	15	345
Occupancy	60				56			

Chapter 20

1. Proposal is acceptable. Contribution £1·05 per sleeper-night.
2. Financially better to open only from April to September. Negative contribution £850 in period October to March.
3. (a) Room takings £120,000; Meals takings £135,000.

$$\frac{£54,000 \times 100}{40} = £135,000.$$

    (b) Food £2·70; labour £2·55; fixed expenses £1·50; variable expenses £1·35; semi-variable expenses £2·85; net profit £1·80

    (c) Proposal is acceptable. Marginal cost £7·80; Contribution £1·20

Chapter 21

3. Break-even point at sales £5,000
4. Break-even point at sales £10,000
5. (a) £2,500   (b) £6,000
6. (a) £14,000   (b) £25,250

Chapter 22

1. (a) Subsidy £2,100 p.a. = £0·042 per employee per day
   (b) Annual cost £4,600 (subsidy £2,100 + luncheon vouchers £2,500)
   (c) £2,038 (assume food cost increases in proportion to number of meals)
   (d) £0·027

2. Pricing policy: add 60% to food cost for each dish.
   Vitamins Ltd employees only: total charges £15,000; subsidy required £8,437 is more than Company is prepared to pay.
   With adjoining factory: total charges £27,000; food cost ($\frac{9}{5}$ × £9,375) £16,875; subsidy required £6,437, which could be shared between the two Companies in ratio 500:400.

3. *Note:* As no information is given regarding food cost, an estimate is required, e.g. assume average food cost is £0·10 per dish. Assumption also required for depreciation, e.g. say 10%.
   (b) If canteen is to break even, gross profit must equal the total of wages £4,264, depreciation (say) £500, replacements £50, and gas £800. So gross profit must be £5,614.
   If food cost is £0·10 per person per day, total food cost per annum will be £7,425.
   Total charges per annum must be £13,039 (£5,614 + £7,425)
   (a) Pricing scheme: each meal charged at food cost plus 75%
   (c) Describe simple operating statement.

Chapter 23

1. Sales Price variance (5p × 9,800) £490 (Fav)
   Sales Volume variance (800 × 45p) 360 (Fav)
   Ingredient Price variance (10p × 250 g × 9,800) (245)(Adv)

   £605 (Fav)

2. Sales Price variance (5p × 1,200) 60 (Fav)
   Sales Volume variance (200 × £1·28) 256 (Fav)
   Ingredient Price variance (£1·20 × 180 kg) (216)(Adv)
   Ingredient Usage variance (50 g × 1,200 × £3·60) 216 (Fav)

   £316 (Fav)

3. Sales Volume variance (1,000 × £1·30)   1,300 (Fav)
   Ingredient Price variance (45p × 600 kg)   (270)(Adv)
   Ingredient Usage variance (50 g × 2,000 × £3·60)   (360)(Adv)
   $$\overline{}$$
   £670 (Fav)

4. (a) Sales 3,000 × £1·50   4,500
       Food cost 3,000 × 200 g × £3·05   1,830

       Gross profit   £2,670

   (b) Sales 4,000 × £1·60   6,400
       Food cost 4,000 × 250 g × £3·16   3,160

       Gross profit   £3,240

5. (a) (i) Sales Volume variance 30 dishes × budget
           G.P. £0·265   7·95(Fav)
       (ii) Ingredient A Price Variance £0·025 × 160 kg   4·00(Adv)
            Ingredient B Price Variance £0·10 × 72 kg   7·20(Fav)
      (iii) Ingredient A Usage Variance

           Actual usage   160 kg
           Budget usage 780 × 200 g   156 kg

                               4 kg × 62½p   2·50(Adv)
           Ingredient B Usage Variance
           Actual usage   72 kg
           Budget usage 780 × 100 g   78 kg

                               6 kg × £1·40   8·40(Fav)

   (b) Budget gross profit   198·75
       Add Fav. Sales Volume Variance   7·95
           Ingredient B Price Variance   7·20
           Ingredient B Usage Variance   8·40

                                                  222·30
       Less Adverse
           Ingredient A Price Variance   4·00
           Ingredient A Usage Variance   2·50
                                        ——
                                                    6·50

       Actual gross profit   £215·80

Index

Also from Heinemann

THE CHEF'S COMPENDIUM OF PROFESSIONAL RECIPES
J. Fuller and E. Renold

This immensely popular book presents essential recipes based on classic traditional methods but simplified and adapted to meet the needs of the busy professional kitchen.

1978 (revised reprint)/434 90586 0

FOOD COMMODITIES
Bernard Davis

Designed to provide students and caterers with a basic knowledge of foods as commodities used in catering, Bernard Davis methodically classifies each food group, their characteristics, methods of production, varieties available, catering uses, storage requirements and scientific and nutritional aspects so that readers can readily identify those areas in which they should be conversant.

1978/434 90297 7

THE LARDER CHEF
M. J. Leto and W. K. H. Bode

'This is the best larder book that has been written since the war . . . suitable not only for cookery students but for people now operating catering establishments. Each section is detailed, easily understandable and readable.'
Catering Times

1975 (second edition)/434 91131 3

PATISSERIE
L. J. Hanneman

Students and practising patissiers will find here the professional knowledge needed to excel in this attractive branch of the baker's art. The many illustrations have been chosen to show finished goods and the techniques used.

1971/434 90707 3

A MANUAL OF STAFF MANAGEMENT IN THE HOTEL AND CATERING INDUSTRY
J. Philip Magurn

Coverage extends from recruitment to industrial relations. Practices described range from induction to wage structuring, motivation to morale, discipline to dismissal, welfare training, communication, counselling and even fire prevention.

1978/434 91198 4